# LIV
# DRUIDRY

*Magical Spirituality
for the Wild Soul*

# EMMA RESTALL ORR

(Bobcat)

**PIATKUS**

PIATKUS

First published in Great Britain in 2004 by Piatkus Books
5, Windmill Street
London W1T 2JA
e-mail: *info@piatkus.co.uk*

A CIP catalogue record for this book
is available from the British Library

ISBN 978-0-7499-2497-3

Printed and bound in Great Britain by
CPI Antony Rowe, Eastbourne

Piatkus Books
An imprint of
Little, Brown Book Group
100 Victoria Embankment
London EC4Y 0DY

An Hachette Livre UK Company

www.piatkus.co.uk

# Contents

## Dedication

*This book is offered with sincerity*
*in honour of my husband, David*
*with whom I have shared 23 years, and*
*without whom I would not be alive*

*I love you*

# First Words

Sitting on muddy-wet grass, curled up in the cold, my arms around my knees, rocking backwards and forwards in the darkness and the wind, I'd heard the voice of a spirit. It was cutting, direct, like a whisper that had glided down, building up speed, to break into sound just beside my head.

*It's not just for you*, it said.

I'd opened my eyes and, for a moment, stared out over the night, the wildness of rocky moorland, vague lines of old stone walls, everything slowly disappearing into darkness. If there had been a glint of light from some scattered farm, it didn't touch my awareness. I simply stared.

It was many years ago, a period of my life when, seeking the deepest teachings with an irrational compulsion, I was living as a wanderer, unwilling to remain anywhere with anyone for more than a day or so. I ate very little, tearing open my soul to taste life in the air I breathed, to find nourishment in scent. Each day I would spend hours in the trance of meditation and connection, dancing to the songs I heard in the trees, flying with skylarks, butterflies, crows, drifting in the silence.

Solitude had embraced my life. Yet clambering down the steep hill paths that night, I knew it was over. A few months later, in ritual witnessed by one of my teachers, I was challenged to make a vow to the ancestors, a vow that he had made in his turn years before: to share the inspiration of this sacred tradition.

Integral to the vow are the many layers of understanding that safeguard the deeper mysteries and the sanctity of the path, yet blazing at the fore there is the commitment to share, to give to others what we have been given, to inspire others because we've been inspired. It's a vow I've now witnessed many people make since that moment when the words were mine: a daunting and powerful vow.

Within a year of the rite I had my first student. My life, which had before been lived in the quiet meadows at the edge of society, became quickly filled with people as I got involved in groups, Groves, then Orders, much to the horror of the wild cat within my soul. In 1997 I wrote a book, *Spirits of the Sacred Grove*, which was published the following year (reprinted as *Druid Priestess* in 2000), and in the years after that two others followed.

My life is still full. I continue to teach students, and to manage Druid organizations and heaven knows what else. Over the past few years I have reclaimed a wider swathe for my own soul learning, taking paths that needed a little more solitude once again, letting my inner cat stretch. It's been an important time. Yet, strolling through a field of barley close to home not long ago, watching the dusk settling, my fingers reaching out to touch the stiffening golden whiskers of the corn, all damp and sun blessed, I was overwhelmed for a moment by the beauty of what I felt and realized that it was time again to share more widely what I have found. I wanted to express what I'd felt unable to express in my first book. I wanted to share what I'd explored more deeply in these last years of profound change.

This book is the result.

It is not an expression of arrogance; I am not here presenting with pride a harvest of knowing. I write instead of my experience as a fulfilment of my Druid vow to share, honoured that I am given the opportunity once again to do so. Upon these pages I hope to scatter words that celebrate the wonder I have felt as I've lived this, my life, walking the sacred path of an ancient tradition. The moments of incredible beauty, of extraordinary vision, have not been given that I might keep them hidden for myself. They are not *just for me*.

I offer my words in the hope that those who read them may glimpse some of the rich inspiration I have felt, breathing it in that they too may feel its natural energy and inspire others in turn. After all, to share freely is one of the most powerful attributes of the human soul.

*guiding me, until I'm aware of my fingertips touching air, then touching nothing, as I slip further, drawn backwards on the dance of the rhythm, back into the mist of darkness, pulling me in, letting me go, pulling me further in.*

*Then the drum is gone ... and there is silence. I'm floating in utter darkness. Disconnected from life, I am free even of the need to breathe or hold myself against the grey weight of gravity. I sense myself in that exquisite moment, the particles of my mind still holding together sufficiently to feel time softly passing, and most exquisitely to feel the embrace of this divine power of endless night.*

*And what an embrace! I feel the strength of her energy holding me, yet not as one who cares. For she is nature as darkness, goddess stretching out through the edgeless universe, filling every atom of my body and mind, the darkness in which tiny glinting specks of light so briefly shine, then disappear. She is not life, nor time and space, but all that exists beyond it, behind it, before and after it. And into her I dissolve, relaxing into her arms, her perfect nature, allowing those sticky particles of self to float free, letting go of me ...*

*It is a song that draws me together again. The words come to me softly, my soul once again gathering itself into form, a chanting melody holding the lines that I hear repeating quietly inside me. For a while I simply listen, but as the song creeps into me I find myself joining in. It is only when I become aware of the forest around me that I realize I am making no sound. I breathe, the scents of leaf mould, early winter mud, filling my lungs, my pores, and leaving my skin listening where I've fallen onto the muddy ground. My body is aching from being motionless for too long.*

*A flutter of feathers wakes me from the stillness, the lingering notes of the chant like a scent in the air. I open my long-closed eyes and look up from the mud, blinking in the dusk, to see a wren, landed on a holly branch a few feet from me. He tilts his head, listening for the thoughts that are barely emerging from the depths of my mind. Hearing my silence, he hops, adjusting his*

# Chapter One

# The Nature of Druidry:
# A priest alone

Let me start with an image.

*The sound is tidal, pulling me in, letting me go. The rhythm clings to the pulse of my blood, holding me utterly, getting louder, slowly rising around me until it's pounding in my heart and bones, becoming all I can feel, pulling me backwards, away into the endless rich darkness I know is waiting just behind me.*

*Then, almost pausing, the sound begins to soften, as if the drum were drifting from me, out into the distance, and I find myself slipping forwards again into the swaying muscles of this physical body, this cramped, cold form I realize is mine, dancing without thinking, riding the pulsing undulation. Then again it rises, then releases me, rises higher, and releases, this ethereal drum* tiny feet on the smooth, dark wood until he is facing me; he dips his head, Need anything? *I smile and shake my head with hardly a movement.* Good, *he whispers. And for a moment we sit together, feeling the holly around us, its rich, clean dark energy protective and sure.*

*Pulling myself up to sit, my body stiff and sore, I reach for an ash twig from the sticks left beside me, and with it I prod the embers of my little fire. I'm not seeking light as the last of the sun leaves the forest, but a wash of warmth would be a rich blessing. The wren watches for a while, then twitches his tail,* Coming? *But I can't; I must gather myself up to get home. He pauses, then flies off, as if with a shrug, and I bend down to send a rush of air into the golden-pink glow, listening to the chant, the drum and the silent darkness, all of which seem carried on the flow of my breath. Flames wake and lick around them, as if dancing to the song.*

*Tugging my coat around me, I push a cold hand into a pocket, finding a small, black incense pouch, and from it I pour into the cupped palm of my hand a pile of herbs, roots and resins, the scent of the essential oils lifting up to my in-breath. I close my fingers around them and call to the spirit of each plant present in the mix,* Sing with me, I ask you, your journey with my journey, in perfect reverence, in honour, *and quietly wait for the feeling of each one to wake to me, waiting for the note of each to hum in my hand. Then, with a prayer of thanksgiving, I scatter the incense onto the fire where it crackles and fizzes, then stills. A swirl of scented smoke rises up and I watch it, feeling the quiet of its dance, resonating as it does with the dark serenity of my goddess, her energy still shining deep inside me.*

*It takes a moment for me to notice the man watching me from across the fire. Partly obscured by drifts of smoke, I'm not immediately sure if he is dead or alive, but he blinks and watches as if he's been there for some time. I nod a greeting; he stares, and as the veil of smoke clears I see his body is still as vague to me as it was behind it.*

Can I help you? *I murmur, not breaking the air with sound. I don't know his face, but I recognize his energy.* Are you waiting for someone at the crossroads? *He doesn't understand.* On the high track? *I've seen a young girl pass that way at dusk on very many nights. She's playful, beautiful, no more than seven years old, often stopping to be with me as I sit by an old beech where two tracks meet. Something inside me connects this grieving, hard-faced man with that laughing child.* Is it her? *I ask.*

She never came home. *His voice is rough, half hiding the burning of his anxiety.*

Your daughter?

*It must be a few hundred years since they both lived, yet somehow I feel he has been up this way seeking her every nightfall for all that time.*

She won't come home, *I say softly.*

*He stares.* I was told you could find 'Oer.

I can. *I sigh. The pain in my leg is getting worse. I can hear the church bells chiming the hour across the village and the valley. I need to pick up my son.* Come back here tomorrow, and we'll find her together. Then you can both go home.

*It's a Thursday afternoon in November, somewhere in the beautiful rural heartland of England. Staggering to my feet, I make my way through the darkening forest, over the meadow and then home, drop my mud-splashed, tatty ritual bag on the mat, pick up my handbag, car keys and phone, and head off into town to meet my son after his class. Driving is always an awkward business after an hour of deep trance and I'm grateful for the headlights that shine through the twilight, revealing the occasional oncoming car slowly approaching down the winding lane.*

*It's an ordinary day.*

⋙◆⋘

I am aware that some people will read my words with a hardened scepticism, considering my perception of both deity and the dead to be delusion. Some might assume that my words are symbolic, a momentary use of fiction in order to present an image. (They aren't.)

Although it may not alter their basic disbelief, many might well find it easier to accept what I have to say if I were writing from the context of a rainforest in central America, southern Africa or south-east Asia, where the woman trancing to the drumbeat she hears in her soul is dark skinned, barefoot, dressed in nothing but a strip of cloth, beads and feathers, with wild black eyes – or even if she were some European apprentice to a 'native shaman' in the American desert. The whole process of waking in the mud to talk with a dead man would somehow fit more easily in a world without television, psychotherapy or civilization.

However, I don't live in such an unfamiliar context. I exist in the midst of Western culture, get red Cotswold mud on my hands and cheeks, and have a VW Polo parked outside my house, and my son's class is in computer technology, IT. But the dead are still the dead, and mud is still mud; and the spiritual tradition that offers me the language with which I understand the world I see, to which I dance and trance and sing, is the tradition of our own ancestral heritage, the native nature religion of the British Isles: Druidry.

In my family, we call it the eleventh percentile. On the basis that human beings are said to have conscious access to only ten per cent of their minds in terms of both memory and sensory processing, when someone consciously perceives more we see it as the quirk of being able to utilize a little of the eleventh percentile. Some call it *second sight*. Many inherit it from a parent or grandparent, both as a physiological state and as an attitude that is willing to accept such an ability. Sometimes it is the trauma of war, severe abuse or an accident, the use of mind-altering drugs, or chronic or acute disease that causes the edges of the mind to break open.

The reason I speak of it right at the start of this book is because there is no way that I could present Druidry other than by expressing my own very personal spiritual vision and practice.

Indeed, as a vibrant living tradition, a path that twists and turns according to each and every moment in time and space, there can be no universal definition of Druidry. As a spirituality based on nature, it presents itself in as wide a spectrum of ways as the Earth herself does, with the sacred relationship between the Druid and the environment differing radically in each place. Harsh landscapes of sea cliffs and mountain storms inspire songs quite unlike those of green fertile meadows and rolling hills, or urban jungles of concrete, street lights and noise, or the moors of purple heather, vast cloudscapes and grazing deer. Furthermore, with roots buried deep in a reverence for the stories and wisdom of the ancestors, Druidry is a spirituality that emerges and grows from a different foundation for each person, according to their own bloodline, family and community history. Diversity is integral to its nature, for it is integral to nature itself.

In search of a pertinent definition of Druidry, many people reach back through millennia of human creativity, finding clues and information in literature, poetry, ancient texts, inscriptions and archaeology, and where the seeker is filled with inspiration he pauses, focusing his understanding of the tradition on that era and location, and the complex web of associations and stories that have grown up around it. As a result, ideas and books on Druidry will always express differing definitions, with some lingering here and some tarrying there.

This book is an expression of my own spiritual path, and as such is vividly coloured by all that has drawn me into the tradition, all that holds and nourishes and inspires my journey as a priest. Mine is not a Druidic practice justified by histories or liturgies, or enacted with pressed white robes, grand titles and clean fingernails.

For me, Druidry is an exuberant celebration of nature's currents, its tides and cycles, an intense journey of exploration and discovery in natural science and emotion. It is about the wild energy of being alive and breathing deeply, right where life shimmers and shudders with its own awareness: in the throes of change, collapse, dying, birthing, waking. It is about the stillness in the pause between ebb and flow. Druidry is about finding the beauty of it, all of it, consciously, wherever we are, in the tranquillity of isolation and in the chattering clutter of the crowd. It is far from a way of seeing or living that could be called conventional. Furthermore, for me, that consciousness is coloured, too, with more than a splash of eleventh per cent perception.

Of course, it isn't necessary to have any kind of second sight to walk the path of the Druid. What the tradition teaches us is to find our own vision and so to develop our own spiritual connection with nature, and that can only be forged with the unsullied honesty of our individuality. That many teachers and priests within the tradition have this vision is not coincidence, however; they see clearly what others are reaching to experience, so are better able to act as guides along the way. Yet, even without the extra quirk of vision, many of those drawn to Druidry have a poignantly high sensitivity of perception and empathy. Life in the *normal* zone is not an option.

We are the strange folk, the edge people.

Druid: the word can be broken down into two Indo-European language strands, the first being the *dru* sound, which can be translated through words found in the languages of many cultures, giving us the idea of *oak* or simply tree, wood or wooden, or going one step further into *portal*, gate or doorway. The *id* or *wid* is the source of many English words, not least wit and wisdom. Both poetically and practicably, we can see the word as a whole presenting an image of one who carries a profound understanding of nature. With the stillness and patience of the ancient oak, yet knowing too the madness of the wilderness and the dark humming forest, he holds a wisdom about the journey of life and death, decay, transition and regeneration, nourishment, healing, change, beauty and pain.

Taking the essence from this etymology, the Druid's work can be seen as that crucial interaction between a people and their landscape, between humanity and the environment. Completing long years of apprenticeship and study, the Druid would principally have been the adviser, counselling a community on the patterns of nature, explaining what was happening and what could happen next. The context has changed, but the work is fundamentally the same. The Druid sees beneath the layers of bark and mud, beneath the masks of glamour and bravado, perceiving the currents of nature itself, the flows of chaos and design, the shimmering of life.

Historically, the word referred to this priest of the land and of the community, and only to the priest, and that sense of Druid as priest remains poignant. Yet a central tenet of modern Druidry is the individual's personal experience of nature as sacred and divine; there is no sense of a priest being *required* as a medium between deity and humanity. As celebrant and guide, the priest's role is still vital, yet much of what she does is facilitating others to walk their own Druid path with confidence and respect. In some senses, everyone in the tradition could say that they are their own priests, and certainly, with the growth of the tradition over the last twenty years, many now call themselves Druids simply by virtue of being students of the tradition, or even by being a part of its spiritual and social community. Understanding the etymology, *Druid* is a beautiful word, a word that leaves traces behind it like a sparkler in the dark, and as such it is for many not a label at all, but an invocation. It is a word used often not as a declaration, but as a sacred reminder and an aspiration.

We may all debate the *need* for a tag to pin to our chest. Few of us would ever like to be classified, fearing the limitations and expectations that can come with any label or name. Words are powerful, nonetheless. As well as being involved with those who stood within the broad spectrum of the Druid tradition, over the twenty years of my training I have studied and performed initiatory rituals with individuals who called themselves *shaman*, and those who used the word Witch, my teachers representing various strands of both traditions. The fact that it was possible to do this expresses how the traditions intertwine. I would not, however, comfortably use the word *shaman* for myself, for to me the Druid is the *shaman* of Britain; alternatively, acknowledging the origins of that word, one might say that shamanism is the Druidry of *its* native land, Siberia. As such, were I to use the word as invocation it would be diluted or twisted. Neither do I consider Witch to be a necessary term for me to use; for as a woman working in a sacred manner with the power of nature, I am naturally a Witch. The invocation can be powerful, and distinctly different from Druid, as I shall explain in a later chapter, but alongside *Druid* it is for me for the most part redundant.

Where we do use the labels, the far-reaching diversity of any nature-based spiritual tradition, and the wide range of roles taken on by practitioners, can make the use of one word feel hopelessly inadequate. Just as anthropologists are realizing that the global use of the word *shaman* is insufficiently descriptive, causing confusion and disrespect, because there are wind singers, bone setters, herbalists, animal healers and spirit talkers, each with their own specialism, so is the word *Druid* in many ways too broad. In the mainstream of the tradition, there are acknowledged bardic and ovatic crafts, yet these too don't describe clearly the difference between those who hold the histories and genealogies, the poets, satirists of word and song, midwives of birth and death, those who work with the energies of land, water, trees, wind and weather, the fire dancers, soul healers, the alchemists of metal, of heart and mind.

None of these skills comes overnight. Druidry is a lifelong apprenticeship to the bumblebee, creeping deep into the heart of the foxglove flower, to the blackbird who sings his ageless song to the beauty of the dusk, to the stream laughing over shifting stones, answering the call of the sea, to the sunlight reflecting golden off windows reflecting windows, to the pebble tumbled smooth by wave upon wave, to the silent dignity of the badger padding home, to the soft flesh of a tiny mushroom pushing twigs aside, to the moon floating in silence upon the water. It sounds magical. Extraordinary. It's simply nature.

Perhaps more than anything, Druidry teaches us to open up our minds – the rational and the irrational – for only then can we discern the patterns, cycles and tides of nature, the energetic flows of all that exists around us and within us. It provides a language with which we can describe our perception and experience of life as something that is more than just physical, yet at the same time it doesn't require us to believe in anything that we cannot perceive or experience.

It guides us not just to acknowledge fully all we know to exist, clearly celebrating scientific discovery and intelligence, but also encourages us to accept the possibility of nature beyond that which we can perceive or prove, beyond the certainty of contemporary scientific vision: it challenges the limits of subjective and human perception, opening our minds to wider potentials. Poignantly it shows us how to accept possibility, diversity, perspectives and realities beyond our understanding, in order that we can walk the paths of our life in harmony instead of conflict and friction.

Instead of faith, what the tradition teaches is trust.

———◆———

*He crouches a little way from me, then sits back on his heels, a thinking frown moving over his beautiful young face before leaning forwards again, completely silently, and for a long while just watching intently.*

*He looks over to where I'm lying in the long grass, his eyebrows raised and a smile on his face.* I can see it, *he says with his eyes, shining with confidence. I beckon him towards me and he creeps over, avoiding the thistles and buttercups.*

*'I saw it,' he whispers, 'just there, like a wavy streak as the bee flew off. It was a red-tailed bumblebee, with pollen all over his face and knees, and he took off, all buzzing in that growly-hum sort of way, but it wasn't the buzz that I saw, it was the whole last five minutes, probably more, but I couldn't know what that was, it was . . . it was . . .' and his words disappear into gestures with his hands that express no more details but are totally filled with his laughter and amazement.*

*I roll over onto my belly and smile at him, all nine years of life bursting through him, so excited to discover words that allow his mind to hold ideas, giving colours and importance to all his moments of experience. His eyes shine with the thrill of sharing and I smile in reply. He doesn't need to know how. Or why. He looks simply for affirmation that his moments were real.*

*His eyes are wide as he looks right at me, 'That's what*

*Druids call the song, isn't it?'*
*I smile again and nod.*
*'Wow,' he murmurs, just before his attention is suddenly*
*captured by the leap of a grasshopper.*

⟹◆⟸

Much of my work as a teacher of Druidry is about affirming the student's own vision, ensuring there is sufficient positive feedback for confidence in their own perception to grow.

Yet there are times when both instinct and intuition can lead us into tangled knots from which it is hard to extract ourselves. We use complicated loops of logic to justify our catatonia, fear based on those first experiences of brutal negation, the dismissive responses of adults or peers that crush our natural ability to trust. As we grow, we learn that anything which isn't obvious and can't be immediately ratified by the whole group is dangerous to admit to. By being ourselves, individual, we risk ridicule and rejection. Yet underneath, for many of us, there remains a layer that still perceives more to life than just the physical matter of flesh, stone and bark. The sense of magic, energy, spirit and mystery doesn't go away.

Because in Druidry we're not required to invest belief in something we can't see or feel, the journeys we make in our spiritual seeking are very like the simple explorations of childhood: with trust held in innocence the child follows his natural curiosity, exploring. Reclaiming that childlike curiosity and trust, the student of Druidry is also searching for deeper experience of life and, because it takes courage to break through the fears and accept what we do perceive or feel, it is that experience which we celebrate: our unique individuality.

Like all spiritualities based on reverence for nature, Druidry is definitively *natural*: it offers us a language and the courage to express what is already within us. Being wholly natural, the basic tenets are incredibly simple.

It is easy for those outside the tradition to judge it on this simplicity, considering that to be all it is, denying the possibility of anything beneath. The priest in deep trance can be seen as a mad woman, spluttering and swaying; the solemn gathering at an old stone circle might seem like costume theatre without a plot; leaving offerings by a tree might look like a dippy-hippy act inspired by too much marijuana and notions of universal love. The motivations for what is actually happening are lost on the outside observer, and particularly where there is a cynicism about anything that reaches into the past, whether it be into the 1960s, 1400s or Romano-Britain. High-tech Western culture invites us to judge any human society that lies outside it – in time or place – as uncivilized.

The English language uses the word *childish* to express derogatory simplicity, yet the natural curiosity and easy explorations of a child are not a reflection of superficiality. Where Druidry is childlike, it is in its uninhibited openness. Its natural simplicity is not unthinking, but uncomplicated. As for being civilized, many Druids would question the implication that all civilization is unequivocally of value. More importantly, however, because Druidry's principles are so natural, its mysteries are that much deeper, for all that is obvious detracts completely from all that is not.

For me Druidry is unquestionably a Pagan religious tradition, and here is another word that implies uncivilized simplicity. In fact, the word *pagan* has been used for centuries to express just such an arrogant judgement. The usual dictionary entry suggests a person who is unenlightened, lacking religious vision or moral fibre. In some cases, such a definition goes hand in hand with a failure to follow one of the main three monotheistic faiths of Judaism, Christianity and Islam. Yet for many millions of people around the world, the tenets of Paganism are exquisite religion: they are not relevant just to Druidry and other British traditions, but also to the spirituality of the Lakota, Navaho, Maya, Maori, Aborigine, Romany, Yoruba and Santeria, to native peoples and nature spiritualities that have been suppressed over centuries. Hinduism, Taoism, Shinto: these are Pagan traditions, too.

It's an important word. Now fairly well accepted in Britain, it is still treated with some suspicion elsewhere, and particularly in the US. Strangely for the 'land of the free' with its constitution of personal rights, the reach of religious fundamentalism leaves those of the old spiritual traditions feeling under more threat than almost anywhere else in Western culture. In the US, using the term *neopagan* seems to soften what are seen as the sharper edges.

However, placing the word back in the cultural context of its root, not only is its full importance revealed, but also it becomes a word to celebrate. The Latin *pagus* is a village or rural community, a *paganus* being someone who lives within that environment; the words compare with *cives* and *miles*, the town dweller and the soldier of Roman society. The key difference here between all three is the authority that ruled their lives. The massive and precisely laid-out hierarchy of the Roman army is well documented; in the cities of the empire, the system of government was clear, with strata of democracy based on social status. The development of human authority into a socially acceptable state was an integral part of the urban empire. Yet, beyond the reach of the towns, the force of authority was still nature. If you weren't in tune with the cycle of fertility, if you weren't sufficiently respectful of the weather or the land, your livelihood was untenable.

Natural law (or lore) is not about that which exists *outside* of humanity, for its flows run through us equally; yet human law focused primarily or solely on human society's needs and cravings, without balancing that current with nature beyond us, is always going to be unsustainable and hierarchical. The pagan knows this. With a small *p*, in modern parlance the word continues to describe those who not only listen to their own instincts and intuitions but look too to the landscape, the environment, the ecology of a place, nature herself, for guidance in every aspect of their lives in order to find that perfect balance.

With a capital *p*, the Pagan is simply one for whom that ancient wordless book of lore, nature, is utterly sacred. Her love of nature has become her spirituality, and as such, she listens more carefully, treads more softly, and celebrates with more exuberance. With this understanding, we can confidently distinguish Druidry as pagan, for it is based on respectful interaction with nature; and with its deepest roots buried in the history of Britain, just as it is the true shamanism of Britain, so is it this island's indigenous Pagan religion.

Along with most Paganisms, Druidry tends to be animistic. While not used as an insult, or inspiring social fear and concern as 'pagan' does, animism – the understanding that all aspects of nature, from pebbles to thunderstorms, have an essential energy or spirit – is clearly another perspective that is associated with tribal or primitive culture. To place it within modern Western culture still seems uncomfortable to many people. Yet this attitude is born of a profound misunderstanding: an arrogance that clearly expresses that ignorance. Where the animist is seen to honour the sun, a river or a mountain, the monotheist compares this with his own worship of a deity that he believes to be superior, more powerful or plausible, whether formless or reflecting human form; the atheist, meanwhile, considers the 'worship' of anything to be ridiculous.

Certainly, animism in societies that remain at a distance from Western culture may still perceive the powers of nature as brutal authority, holding their force at bay, managing the threat to their fragile sustainability with prayers and sacrifice. However, animism within societies that have evolved through times of ease and comfort is not based on the same pleas and deals of appeasement. It is responding to quite different concerns.

The animist in modern Druidry doesn't idolize or worship anything. Instead, she seeks to *rebuild* a language of respect in a world that has been desecrated by human abuse. The perspective that allows this is the acknowledgement that every thing in nature is filled with the pure energy of life: its own spirit humming. Every thing is perceived as individual, existing within its own ecosystem of symbioses, connected and yet unique. Every thing is moving through its own journey from emergence to evanescence, singing its own song of living and dying, of identity and intention.

Druidry is not a theology that requires belief. It is a perspective of the world that can be upheld by science and philosophy in rigorous debate, breaking up the semantics of defining this or that, coming to rest on solid ground balancing in one hand *energy* and in the other *poetry*.

For many, it is a vision that is utterly *natural*. It can feel like the reawakening of the child's perspective within us, where all we see around us is new and utterly amazing. Because we aren't pulling things into little pieces in order to classify and understand every thread and twitch, it all feels miraculous, magical, beautiful. It fills us with wonder, and with the excitement and the open inner calm that comes with that wonder.

Far from being uncivilized, Druidry as a Pagan spirituality, based so completely on animistic vision, is in reality both modern and poignantly relevant to the world today.

―――――◆――――――

*A circle of figures – I see them silhouetted against the twilit sky. They seem to glide instead of walk, their legs and human movements obscured by robes that sweep down to the dry ground. The fire hovers in the air like some magical illusion, utter darkness beneath it, the light now and then glowing on faces as one or another moves, raising hands in invocation or prayers I cannot hear.*

*A gust glances off my wing, lifting the tip and, conscious of feathers, muscles outstretched, I adjust my course again, soaring high on the wind, watching. Yet the wind's current leads me down towards them, or is it my intent to hear? There is a murmuring in the wind, their feet on the roughness of the grass, their limbs slow as if arduously pushing through this shimmering night air. Pausing my breath for that last instant to descend quietly, slowly, I land on a standing stone, one of the dozen that encircle them, and I listen.*

*Then, in the beat of my next breath, balancing, I am pulled into song . . .*

*The pain shudders through me as I open my eyes, feeling myself again in damp, cold human form. I feel as if I've fallen out of the sky, suddenly completely out of synch with the ritual I'm in the midst of. I look around at the others, their eyes still closed, as their voices, filled with human breath, wash the circle with waves of music. Most of them seem so strangely solid, so present, faces flushed with cold yet warm with determination, with physical flesh and blood, with focus.*

*I open myself to breathe the air, the skies, once again, conscious of the vague figures of ancestors watching, conscious of an old raven perched on the stone behind me. Or is that me . . . For a brief moment I have two sets of eyes, one watching the rite with a distant empathy, the other, sharper and less colourful, observing it with detached curiosity. Then, something changes, the energy of the group, and I shiver in my robe. The song is finished and, as the energy of the group silently turns to me and waits, I remember why we are here.*

*I close my eyes. The half crescent of the moon lingers in my mind's eye; I focus my soul on the energy, relaxing, exhaling, opening myself utterly to the thread of silver light upon dark stone, and it pours down into me, into the bowl of intent crafted of my unspoken words, the bowl of my prayer. And as it fills, my soul lifts, and this time I speak my prayer aloud, my voice drifting onto the breeze that is playing in the dark air, 'Touch me, my lady, show me the flow of this, show me the truth . . .'*

*And in that moment I feel the raven behind me move forwards into my body; I sense her warm down feathers and rib bones, then her wings half open briefly as she settles, and I feel the strength of her shoulders, broad and pushing slightly forwards. I relax, accepting, finding the way that we fit, and she rises up into my face, looking through my eyes at the gathering. She feels so dispassionate compared with the vulnerability of the aching me beneath human skin. I relax, exhaling once again, and as her consciousness touches mine, her visions flow into my mind.*

*I have flown out to the edges of the forest, looking down from above, at the contours of the valley, the curve of the hills, the gaping wound of the quarry glaring bright and barren beside the soft darkness of the trees. I've seen the track beneath the canopies that marks the extent of their plans for expansion, for destruction. I have felt uncertainty shuddering and chattering through the forest itself, the energy of their intention creating instability and change. Quietly, I tell the story to those gathered around the fire, relating the visions of the raven within me. In that acutely sensitive place, I'm aware of each word given out, ideas painted into sentences like little piles of stones quietly shown, passed around. And when I'm done, any words still left in my soul I scatter over the ground in breath and thanksgiving. My part is played and, although none of us moves, internally I step back.*

*There is silence amongst us. The moon's light and weight still fills my soul. There is nothing to do but let the moments roll through us.*

*Another steps forwards. He makes no movement, but I sense the sway of his robe and I smell badger. His voice barely breaks the stillness. 'This is what I saw,' he says softly, and his words, mud-scented, rise around us.*

*I wonder, as the flames flicker in the black-iron of the fire dish, how many times priests like us have gathered in this circle of stones. For over four thousand years the stones have stood here, slowly slipping, falling, moving in time, so smoothly grey, silently listening. How many times have they heard visions told, as guardians of the land have come together, striving to understand, to protect . . .*

———◆———

In every culture, in every part of the world, human beings have reached out to the very limits of their knowledge to comprehend the wild powers of nature. Since first we found a consciousness that allowed us to perceive ourselves, to see connections in the world around us and to envisage what might lie beyond, we have sought ways to alleviate the stress of mortality.

Many thousands of years ago, the forces of fire, darkness, death and rage, thunder, flood, birth and blood, would have been paramount in the lives of our ancestors, as would the mountains and deep caves, the forests that stretched forever. These powers were the divine forces, the gods who held sway, ruling with mystery and absolute authority, and through our quest to understand emerged the earliest religions.

As humankind began to settle, beginning to grasp the cycles necessary for farming, we can imagine them experiencing the glimmers of a sense of control over nature. Fire may have become a part of daily life, but through the long years of early agriculture, fertility and lactation, rain, sunshine, warmth and famine, and the surge of growth and harvest became the mysterious powers of nature most important in our Neolithic minds.

For thousands of years, the curiosity and adaptability of the human mind had driven us to explore every aspect of our environment, and all through those millennia religion was inseparable from nature. Yet as man found ways to affect the world he lived in, so his attitude changed. Instead of living *with* nature, he was discovering how he could overcome its dominance; finding comfort and certainty, he felt the gods were not so powerful. Learning how to tame metals, especially the magical black iron that lent such a potency to his natural aggression, he became stronger than he'd ever been before. As human ability to affect and control increased, so the gods of nature *as an authority* were diminished.

Into their place stepped the far more human authority that was the single god of evangelical religions like Christianity. There developed the concept of one man in charge, the alpha male at the top of the tree, and a new account of the world was described, in which creation was a resource provided for the sole benefit of humanity. Through a steady flow of hand-picked prophets, these new ideas were given as laws to humanity. The old Paganisms were pushed back into the far reaches of rural society where nature was still untamed, still wild and brutal.

Paganism and pagan practice started to find itself persecuted. The traditions that had been a natural part of life were declared unnatural, misguided, evil, and those who held the knowledge of natural lore − whether used in medicine and caring, farming, metalwork or love − were suspected or indicted of misdemeanors against the whole community. Those who had power over the people used the religious hierarchy of the Church to add weight to their authority, suppressing further this force of nature they feared.

As a people under threat, those of the old tradition used their knowledge in their own defence. The understanding of connectivity, the beauty of each individual song, became the means of fighting back. Pagan traditions around the world became heavy with the craft of cursing and self-protective malevolence, and because of this many of them still experience both persecution and the prejudice of negative associations. For centuries Druidry was equally oppressed. Over the past century, however, it has not been burdened so heavily with the connotations of satanism and sorcery: it is now generally believed to have been destroyed during the Roman occupation of Britain nearly two thousand years ago. Considered by some to be a valid part of our British or European heritage, modern Druidry is more often thought of as ridiculous and hopelessly inauthentic.

Personally, I feel no need to validate my spiritual practice with historical justifications or authentication, nor to whitewash its history into something bloodless and acceptable to the modern palate. What I practise and teach is the living expression of a tradition whose roots stretch back through many millennia, a Pagan religion that is coloured and scented by the particular landscape and history of these islands of Britain, and the adventures of its people. Its validation comes solely from its effectiveness, now, as ever, offering a language with which we can describe – and so hold and develop – an honourable and sustainable relationship with nature and the experience of life as more than just flesh and mud, a language that doesn't require us to flay the mysteries with proof, a language that allows a foundation from which we can reach for ecstasy: soul-deep peace and satisfaction.

I don't claim my practice to be identical to that of a Druid priest five millennia ago, or two millennia, or five hundred years, or even ten. If I were performing the rites of my forebears in Romano-British culture, most of my actions would no doubt be considered outlandish, ethically dubious, possibly illegal and – most importantly – irrelevant or inappropriate. Like most Pagan spiritualities, Druidry is an *oral* tradition, and one of the definitive characteristics of any oral tradition is that it is not held within the limited context of one moment, one idea, one mind. With no books that hold dogma, liturgy, tracts of ethics or authority, the student and priest alike seek out all they need for each new moment, each new situation, finding understanding in nature's flows of energy, finding answers in relationships. Evolving through millennia before it was documented by Classical writers, changing still with each new day, each new telling of a tale, each new apprentice listening, each new teaching shared, Druidry is always what it needs to be. That is its nature; that is nature.

To question whether the tradition has an unbroken history reveals a misunderstanding about what Druidry is. As the relationship between the people and the land, set within a language of honour and spiritual respect, it not only allows, even encourages, but also *requires* us to adapt each and every teaching to the perfect relevance of the situation we are experiencing, here and now. Druidry could not be lost. Farmers I've met, conservative Protestant men in their fifties and sixties, have watched me make ritual and approached me afterwards to laugh and wonder if perhaps they've been Druids all their lives without knowing it ... 'You know, you're right, when I'm out there looking up at the clouds and I need a dry day, I don't pray to God, I'm praying to the clouds, the wind, trying to understand.'

The issue of Druidry's legitimacy is helped by its realism: there is no documented account of its long history (there are some beautiful forgeries and poetic claims, but nothing proven or provable). Academics, sceptics and journalists are amazed when I laugh, admitting that we make it up as we go along, yet this is the nature of the tradition. Every text, ancient and modern, every archaeological discovery, is explored with studious discipline, but not for fine-tuning our authenticity: our quest is for inspiration to enable us to live in sacred relationship now, and that inspiration is found in history, in mythology and in nature.

That is not to devalue what continuity there is. When the Roman occupation of Britain began in the first century CE, the incoming force was as polytheistic and animistic as the native population. Significantly more urban in mentality and with a monetary lore that held far less sway in Britain than in other parts of the Roman empire, the Roman determination to dislodge the Druids was not religious; it was purely about practical power and wealth. The Druids had a great deal of authority in society at the time, holding control over land rights, trade routes, inheritance claims, education and so on; the Roman invasion didn't annihilate the religion, it simply kicked its priests off their political perch.

Certainly the persecution and loss of status pushed the tradition into the shadows, and the brutality of the Roman attempt to destroy those who wouldn't cooperate was horrific. However, looking at religions that have held political power over centuries, losing their spiritual integrity, ruled by force and not mystery, I'm not sure the Druids' loss of authority was altogether unpropitious. It is idealistic to imagine that a Druidry today, with an unbroken history of political power, would be any less rapacious and selfish than any other force. The spirituality would have been lost; power too easily corrupts.

Without the Druids in control, continental influences flowed into Britain, particularly after the fall of the Roman empire, with northern European and Germanic peoples moving onto the islands, yet Druidry continued, adapting, absorbing, evolving and underpinning our society, ever rooted as that sacred relationship between the people and the land.

Bardic colleges, which held much of the oldest teachings of Druidry, albeit gradually Christianized, continued throughout the medieval period, the last closing in Scotland in the nineteenth century. Indeed, although Christianity deleted and diluted much of the old mythology, it acknowledged the power of Paganism, taking its symbolism and language, transmuting the old festivals into saints' days and holy days, from Midwinter's celebration of rebirth to Easter eggs and harvest rites. In my old local parish church, a Norman building that has been renovated in local stone half a dozen times over the last eight hundred years, and that is rich in fossils and history, there are hidden Green Men, forest figures, faces adorned with leaves. From around Midsummer and the cutting of the first hay, the floor of the church is strewn with freshly mown grass for three long weeks: utterly beautiful, aromatic and pagan.

Artists, poets, historians, musicians and songsmiths, seeking beauty and inspiration in the environment and upon currents of time, have been holding the sanctity of the tradition for centuries. Spiritual healers, herbalists, midwives, mediums, geomancers, water diviners and metal smiths, all these too hold the ancient mysteries that were once learned and taught by the Druids of our heritage. The magic of rituals no longer performed is expressed in the themes and visions of children's tales, in folklore, ale songs, superstitions and mythologies. We can add to the flow of its history the rich heritage of Druidic teachings that has always run through families and lines of apprenticeship, whether focusing broadly on the tradition or along specialist lines, such as earth magic, divining, healing or smithing.

This is how the tradition has survived, moving like a river through the landscape of time, flowing between old banks that are always slowly shifting, breaking now and then to create new channels of flow, exploring new possibilities, irrigating new meadows, sometimes even disappearing to seep through underground rocks to emerge again, clearer, cleaner, ever rich with life.

Where gaps remain in our vision as we walk the path today, where we crave inspiration and ancestral wisdom, we are guided to study the archaeology, reaching back into the Neolithic era, so gaining understanding that enriches our modern practice of the tradition. It is a tradition that is soundly based on the value of study, and we read not only the newly published books, but all there is in terms of literature, from Classical texts and medieval poetry, folklore and mythology, through to the mysticism, magic, metaphysics and cultural revivals of the nineteenth and early twentieth centuries. As individuals we learn, finding inspiration for ourselves, walking with our own feet and making our own footprints.

*Living Druidry* is the title of this book. It's an expression I've used for some years, and the title of the course I teach in the Cotswolds here in the heartland of Britain. It expresses two things: firstly, the fact that Druidry does still exist, and is evolving and growing. As a British Paganism, its community is growing faster than almost any other spiritual tradition. Secondly, the title declares that Druidry must *be lived*, for pondering it as a theory, an ideology, is all but useless.

The next chapter offers a starting point. As we explore the ideas that make up the nature of Druidry, our focus adjusts, our worldview changing. The landscape around us becomes more vibrant and rich with life. Preparing for the adventure, we first seek out a place where we can place our feet firmly on the ground.

# Chapter Two

# Finding Focus:
# A place to begin

The world is divided into two kinds of people: those who have an interest in spirituality and those who don't. Trauma, near-death experience, grief or disease may just wake an interest in spirituality in someone who had no interest in it before, but without the kick of the extraordinary you can't provoke spiritual curiosity. To this half of society, the others who spend long hours in theological discussion or deep meditation, let alone in the apparent futility of prayer or ritual, will always seem bizarre, objects of ridicule and bewilderment. They will appear simply to be seeking ways in which to justify the existence of the implausible.

Druidry lies like a headland that stretches out from that landscape of spirituality into the seas of not believing. For, as I have said before, it is truly not necessary to believe in anything in order to walk the path of the tradition; as a result, some people define it not as a spirituality at all, but as a philosophy, a way of life not incompatible with modern science, reason or humanism. I myself do use the word *spirituality*, for a fundamental tenet of the tradition inspires us to recognize *spirit*: not as something supernatural, requiring blind faith or eleventh percentile vision, but as the pure energy of life, powerful and sacred.

Nor does Druidry support the need for an external or social affirmation about what is reality, what is truth and what is imagination. Instead, there is the acknowledgement of each individual's subjective experience of the world, and an understanding that, based on their own perception and acceptance, that experience might well be radically different for each and every one of us.

Although we may find common ground and a place where we can share, to the Druid it is understood that this is possible not necessarily because of any similar experience but through the value of a shared language, the language of our spirituality. The need for our common ground to go deeper than this is not essential in Druidry, nor is it expected. The diversity of utterly individual experience only adds to the richness of the living tradition.

Our understanding of Druidry, then, may be very individual, and what makes us the kind of person who leans towards spirituality at all may not be entirely a matter of choice. Once we are on that road, however, what motivates our spiritual questing is quite often similar. Whether it is a vague curiosity that moves us to pick a book off a shelf, or an overwhelming compulsion that draws us into the priesthood, what inspires us is a craving for peace, the yearning for an inner freedom, the longing for a soul-deep certainty, for absolute stability. We are seeking an understanding about life that will ease the anxiety of mortality, of being human.

For myself, the fuel of the quest has always been focused on the motivation to live. When I was first seeking, I wasn't so interested in finding an answer that allowed life to make sense; I just wanted life to be *worthwhile*. As is the case for most highly sensitive children, my first score years were fraught with the crises of living in a world that seemed noisy and brutal; unable to play with the other kids, I was the observer, sitting alone, learning how to be the outsider. On top of the normal confusion of sensory input that so disorientates the very sensitive, my father's bloodline had gifted me with a more serious physical disorder: nerves acutely overreacting left me sleepless and in chronic pain. By the time I was fifteen, I had perfected the guise of the alienated freak. It kept everyone at a comfortable distance, allowing me the solitude and quiet I needed to deal with the pain in silence. By sixteen, I'd discovered drugs that both facilitated self-destruction and numbed the screaming of my nerve endings.

A highly toxic but effective blend of influences hurled me through those years, the hunger for control driving me to read philosophy from Plato to Wittgenstein, together with the Vedas, the Koran and every other sacred text I could find. The exploration led me into the study of Witchcraft and the quest for power, while the desperation to lose control drove me deeper into drugs and subcultures along the edges of society. I met death a number of times, sometimes actively calling her towards me, sometimes leaping in terror when she emerged out of thin air.

Serious self-destructive tendencies are not best served by the kind of study I was pursuing. At the age of twenty-one, I was seething with enough power and desolation to make suicide for the first time a fully viable option, yet I also had enough power of reason to realize there was actually an alternative: not continuing half alive, crawling through life stupefied on my own blend of pain and drugs, but beginning to live, fully awake and with all my wits about me.

That was the place where I began: one February night, on a dirty, cold street corner somewhere in south-west London, in the acrid orange glow of the street lights, my mind crawling quietly, wide-eyed, out of the landfill site that had been my life.

I had throughout my twenty years had visions, the eleventh per cent offering me a way of seeing the world in all its intensity of beauty and horror. I had experienced the kicking power of deity, I'd seen the spirits of the dead and the fey, and I knew what it was like for my mind to be separate from my body. I had even had extraordinary experiences of what might be called religious revelation: the entirety of human experience in a tear rolling down the gaunt cheek of a starving street child, the brilliance of universal energy shining in a raindrop in sunlight, the utter insignificance of my life shaken by the growling thunder of an earthquake ... all moments that shattered the limitations of my adolescent mind.

This beginning, however, wasn't about some magical experience or mystical consciousness whereby I suddenly realized that life was more than I'd imagined. It was a decision.

Now, in my work and in the world about me, I watch others meandering around that same place, aware or unaware of what they are doing. Life does seem easier when we soften it with our socially acceptable pacifiers – alcohol, a little marijuana, animal fats and high sugars, and passive screen entertainment. Yet, now and then, someone will wake up and realize that they are unhappy and getting nowhere. Slowly, finding the courage and the stillness, they reach the point where they can step forwards and make that decision: to live.

———⊳◆⊲———

*The smell is so familiar. It evokes in me that familiar response, too, the instinctive mix of revulsion and curiosity, and I watch as she murmurs her prayers, her voice still shaking, '. . . to find peace, release, to find release, for both of us . . .' A pool forms, rich, shining deep red, before seeping into the earth as a patch of dark. She watches it too, and for a long moment the two of us are quiet.*

*Setting down the painted jar beside her, she allows herself to fall from crouching, sitting down heavily on the damp ground. And I wait. The soft call of an owl touches the breeze; I look up through grey branches into the winter-lit sky.*

*Earlier, in the quiet of her sitting room, we'd spoken of what she wanted to do. There had been no reason for the miscarriage, nothing anyone was willing to declare or explore, and she had sat in her grief, in the void of futility.*

'I'm sure it was a boy.'

I nodded. It was vague, a blurred image, mostly just a change of light, but I felt sure of the presence of a young man standing beside her. His hand touched her shoulder; she breathed in deeply and sighed. For a moment I wondered if I might tell her that I could see him. But she was fighting tears, needing strength more than comfort, and as she shook her head with determination I could see that, even though she wasn't aware he was there, she was shaking the spirit off herself. I watched him step back.

Was it your decision to pull out? I wondered if he'd hear me or take any notice.

The energy changed as he turned towards me.

. . . wrong time . . . was all I heard.

Will you come again? She so desperately wants a child.

The shimmering image visibly dulled.

I wished that I could tell her she'd be pregnant again in no time, that it was simply bad timing, but his clear withdrawal from my question almost implied the converse.

She looked up and I smiled tenderly, and watched as she grew noticeably stronger the further the spirit backed away. She picked up her mug of tea at around the moment when I could no longer feel his presence at all, and drinking the last of it she said, 'I'll get that jar.' She cleared her throat, steadying her voice. 'We should go out before it rains.'


As she'd poured her blood onto the mud, I had felt her releasing some of the pain. It had risen off her like a sweat evaporating in the morning sunlight, the tightness of her womb-grief silently lifting. It would take some time, but the process had begun.

Now I sit down beside her here on the cold ground.

'I reckon,' she says softly after some time, 'he just changed his mind.'

I nod.

The little owl calls again, and this time a reply comes from across the forest. The light is fading, dusk closing in. We sit there for a long while, just watching the night falling.

Then she whispers, 'I don't know if I ever made that choice.'
'To live?'

'Yes,' she turns to me briefly but, deep in thought, her eyes drift again. She picks up a dry twig and rubs it with her fingers. 'I mean, maybe we all need to make the decision to be born. I've just . . .' she shrugs '. . . pissed my life away, getting blown by the slightest influence but never taking responsibility for a damn thing, never making anything happen for me, never actually . . .'

'Stepping into your own shoes?'

She smiles, nods, yes, still looking at the twig in her hand. 'So I'm going to do it.'

'When?'

'Now?'

'How?'

She stands up, 'I dunno. You're the priest. Tell me what to do.'

I look at her, OK. 'The next step you take is your own choice.'

She closes her eyes and breathes in. Then shakes her head, 'Oh hell, bugger, bugger! Maybe I don't want to. What if I don't want to?' Her voice trembles, 'Bobcat? He didn't want to. What if I don't want to either? It's too bloody hard to do it half the time. It's not easy being alive, you know! Bloody hell!'

'If you don't want to, then don't.'

She opens her red, grief-smeared eyes and glares at me, don't be so bloody irritatingly calm! But then sighs, pulling her hair away from her face, and stares into the forest air before her. And she murmurs, 'OK. This is my last breath,' and very consciously she fills her lungs again, exhaling through lips that almost whistle, until she's pushing out the very last.

And I watch her breathlessness. It is empty. Timeless. I feel the energy of the earth beneath us more acutely, feeling the sky falling silently with twilight all around us.

Then she breathes, suddenly gasping, then leaping into the quiet. It makes me laugh with surprise. She's yelping and waving her arms, and for a moment it's like fireworks, then brightly coloured bits of paper wildly scattered and falling over grief-murky

*water. Then almost as suddenly there's stillness again.*
   *She breathes gently, tired but stronger.*
   *'All right then. Let's go and do it. Let's bloody live . . .'*

⟫━━◆━━⟪

Druidry is very much about that decision. Guiding us to heighten our awareness of the natural world both around us and within us, it shows us just how we can live life to the full. This is not about a blaze of glory, but about a life that is holistically sustainable, where we are sufficiently connected to be naturally responsible. But how?

In tune with most mystical spiritual traditions, one of the key teachings of Druidry is perfect presence. Instead of spending our lives in a mist of memories, doing all we can to hold onto and recreate past experiences, and ever reaching into the future, clinging to dreams, shying away from fears of what might or might not happen, we bring our focus into the here and now. We self-locate: we find ourselves in time and space.

It's an elusive place, the present, for immediately we catch a moment it disappears into the past. Immediately we grasp where we are it's different, the currents of nature ensuring perpetual change. But we aren't taking photographs, snapshots for the collection; we are learning to live, and to do so means learning how to stay in that flow of evanescent instants.

It may come in brief glimpses, but with practice we can extend those twinklings into minutes, spreading them into hours, until it becomes a part of our natural perception. Such presence offers endless opportunities for deeper experience, richer connection, serenity. It isn't about meditating with eyes closed and focus held somewhere within; awareness of the moment is about being wide awake, conscious of the vibrancy of life energy as it flows in time, through our own bodies and through the environment of our home. Being present is about the immediacy of relationship as spirit encounters spirit, body touches body, feet on grass, fingers on wood, skin on skin. Truly there, we can fully share the experience of the moment, and so respond both respectfully and with poignant relevance.

Being present is not about the hurry of doing this and doing that, but about exploring the sensations of being alive. This isn't passive, a way of living that is little more than a perpetual shuddering of reactions, unaware of the future, forgetful of the past, uncaring of those around. Instead of *doing* life, presence allows us to *be* alive, offering a clarity that enables us to respond actively with care, choosing our footsteps upon the path all the way. Presence evokes in us wonder. It might be said that only by achieving a state of present focus can we see the incredible nature of life, and it is this wonder that inspires us to call life 'sacred'.

To the Pagan, all of nature is sacred. It is not possible to say that one thing is more or less sacred than another, whether we are referring to clear rivers or swamps, cockroaches or butterflies. We may treat one thing as sacred and forget another, because it takes many years to achieve the ability to live in a sacred manner, but that is a reflection of our human limitation and not of the world around us. The energy of life, as it moves through stones two hundred million years old, as it moves through mayflies, brief lives flickering in the wind, is still life, pure energy and utterly amazing. It is the sense of wonder evoked by the pure magic of *life energy* that causes us to call it sacred, and so to use the word *spirit*.

We perceive this spirit or life energy in a number of different ways. We can ponder on it with our intellect, accepting and agreeing that a tree exists as a complex skein of energy on a subatomic level, and experiencing mental satisfaction in grasping the science. We might feel emotionally connected to the tree because of what it means to us, for example as beauty or familiarity, sensing its life force nourishing our lives and our environment. We may even, with a little eleventh per cent vision, see the shimmering of this energy as a haze of colour around its canopy against the sky. We can touch it and feel the warmth of its physicality. However, only when we are able to relate to the tree through a consciousness of our *own* spirit do we feel that deep connection.

Becoming aware of our own spirit is an important starting point in the craft of Druidry, and in this quest one of the first steps we take, paradoxically perhaps, is to reawaken our physical senses. Either they are numb through lack of conscious use, the apathy of no longer wishing to be fully aware of life, or they have become muddled and dull with constant distraction, the alertness provoked by fear leaving us exhausted and confused. Clarifying our senses, we remove the layers of blindfolds, bandages and padded gloves that have kept us detached.

We do it gently, slowly.

We begin by playing with touch, taking into our hands objects we've not consciously held for a long time, using our fingertips to explore, stroking, discovering again the qualities of texture, friction and softness. With eyes closed, perhaps in the dark, and without listening, we learn again how to touch and feel, releasing ourselves into the experience.

We might find some unusual items, or have a friend or teacher put into our hands things we have no knowledge of, but it is equally important to reconnect with the world we're familiar with. The textures and shapes of our home, the place where we work, the food we eat, the clothes we wear, plants and trees, the people we live with, all these we learn how to wake to again through touch, just touch.

This isn't something we can do overnight; I give this one apparently simple exercise to students to focus on wholly for at least a few months before adding any other ideas to the pot. With that awareness rekindled, we turn our focus to the earth beneath us, at first in that very physical way of exploring with our fingers, hands and toes, going barefoot and getting muddy or dusty, and dirty. Shoes are such effective blindfolds for the feet!

We might back up our exploration with our minds, feeding our imagination by reading books about local geology, geography and water courses, finding the ancient stories of the land itself. We can explore our own attachment to it through history, memories, familiarity. Only then, when we have a strong sense of our connection physically, emotionally and mentally, might we extend our practice into the spiritual.

Sitting undistracted, we learn how to do something that will become an integral part of life in the tradition: we feel the spirit of the earth. Using our own blend of sensitivity and imagination, we open our awareness to its energy. We may perceive it in colours, temperature, its presence shimmering all around us. Taking our consciousness down into the ground, we discover a profound feeling of being rooted, emotionally and physically: settled, stable and unshakeable.

Perhaps most exquisitely, we feel acceptance. No longer skittering on the surface, we experience a deep sense of belonging. In a relationship that has evolved over millions of years, we come to realize just how wholly we are connected to the earth, becoming aware of how it holds us and, consciously allowing ourselves to be nourished by it, we breathe in its spirit. Yet, shining with this rich energy, we are also filled with the energy that the earth has inspired in us. It has woken us to our own power. We feel our own spirit.

With this sensation of spirit, of life shining through us, we are guided in the tradition to go back to exploring touch, this time feeling with fingertips, toes, belly and lips that shimmer with spirit. We walk on the ground, on grass and mud, tarmac and stone, we hold the apple, stroke the bark, touch the cat, nose to nose, kiss the belly of a lover, feel the breeze on our skin. The sensitivity has intensified, and we stand more strongly in the present, allowing the sensations to flow through us undiluted by expectation, utterly awake to what we feel.

In our search for presence, then, touch is our first focus.

---

*Pushing my hands through it where I sit, the pressure against my skin, I feel it responding to the movement. Like something*

*between water and air, it glimmers around me, a vast pool of
fathomless grey a foot or so deep. My eyes closed, I let my hands
fall to the ground, and though my fingers hit the dust of the
paving, my soul extends them into the deep, grey energy. Very
different from the mud of home, the scent is slightly bitter, the
pulse a good deal faster. I wriggle my spirit-fingers in the solid
earth, damp, dark compacted soil, shards of stone, brick rubble and
twisted roots.*

*The cold breeze touches my face, whispering,* Breathe!

*Prompted to open my eyes, I look up at the winter-bare tree
whose branches reach over me; hard to identify in the half-light of
this city garden, it feels like a hybrid rowan, strong and naive
compared with many in the wild. I lift a hand and touch its
smooth silver bark, feeling its spirit slip over my skin, letting my
fingers move within its energy.*

*A cat lands on the high brick wall, pausing to watch me before
dropping silently and disappearing into the dark flower bed, thick
as it is with the dead remains of last summer's herbaceous growth.
He emerges from beneath the brittle stalks of a hydrangea, hungry
with curiosity but too nervous to come forwards. I watch as his
tail twitches in this pool of shimmering grey, and I breathe, the
fluttering gusts of cold wind, the air that touches my face, so soft
and chilly and smelling of the city.*

*I must do what I came to do.*

*I get to my feet and walk out into the middle of the courtyard
garden. The cat shies away as I close my eyes. The paving stones
suddenly irritate me and I pull off my boots and socks, the cold
shock of the stone for a moment spinning me dizzy. I breathe,
feeling the energy, and with every out-breath I relax a little
further, sinking, consciously unfurling my soul's roots into this
disturbed ground, extending the tap root that runs from my spine
deep into the compacted earth beneath me, reaching further with
prayers until I can secure it about solid rock.*

*Then, with each exhaled breath of relaxation, I stretch out my
wider web of roots, the little feelers on each thread quivering,
reaching out deep and far in every direction, seeking out moisture*

*and nutrients, caverns and toxins, exploring the darkness with
every nerve awake. And with each in-breath comes a little more
understanding, the flow of history spreading out beneath me,
touching my mind, my soul, wordlessly.*

*With edgeless feet, I move over the stone, my fingers sensing
and intensifying the tiny differences in flow beneath me. Then I
hit something new: it feels clearly as if the ground has fallen away
beneath me and I open my eyes and check the paving stones,
confirming that they are level. I step back and then forwards
again, feeling the dip and the rush of energy, dark and dirty. I
want to shake it off my fingers, but I turn and find its bank,
walking back and forth, mapping the length of it from the far wall
over towards the house, and when I have it clear in my mind I
fully open my eyes, integrating what I have sensed below with
what I see above.*

*The patio door is open and the silhouette of a man looks out
at me.*

*His voice is tired but gentle, 'What did you find?'*

*I show him the current of earth energy I'd felt so acutely. It
runs under the beautifully ornate cast-iron bench beneath a
struggling rose arbour. 'Do you use the seat?' I ask.*

*He half laughs, but with sorrow, admitting to another part of
his life that isn't running to plan, 'No, no one ever does. Except
the cat.'*

*I reach down and pick up my boots. 'Let's see if it runs
underneath your daughter's room.'*

---

As well as nourishing us more fully, our ability to root allows us a
clearer sense of how earth energies differ, depending on the rock,
the soil depth and fertility, moisture and so on. It is an awareness
that gives us a better understanding of where we feel comfortable
and secure, and where we don't. We are not only reaching into the
land, finding consciousness of its spirit, more acutely feeling our
own, but also observing its effects and relationships around us. It

may be that some places are not healthy for human beings, somehow jarring our energy, making us sluggish or sick, irritated or anxious.

There are places on the earth where the energy is high, sharp and clear, still flowing down rivers of fluid rock, along the courses of lava flows, cascading down fissures, molten waterfalls in the dark roaring silence below. There are places where energy is stagnant, where flows have become trapped, curling around onto themselves in eddies and pools, slowing to a standstill. There is water beneath us too, rivers, lakes and deep still pools, water that may never reach the light of day, yet holds within it the richness of natural minerals, of human pollution, and aeons of history.

Animals and insects respond to the different energies intuitively, choosing places to sleep, nest, mate, feed and fight. That cat in the city garden, a hundred per cent predator, was at ease in the high energy that was so negatively affecting the family. Plants and trees reflect the energies through rates of growth and decay, curves, twists, mutations, health and fruitfulness. It is clear that the spirit of one place will nourish one creature while being harmful to another.

So we learn to feel our own reactions, as the earth spirit touches our spirit, and we watch others' reactions, the interplay of spirits, energies, currents meeting and changing; and acknowledging the variations, we make decisions about our own human paths, with relevance and with reverence.

For those in the tradition who go further into the study of earth, there are ways of following these tracks and flows, sending moments of consciousness along them, thoughts and intentions. Some have found ways to change the course or current of a flow, using song, standing stones or – more coarsely – metal stakes. There are times when such action feels to me both powerful and valid, and to be a part of such a rite is an exquisite honour. There are times, however, when the shifting of earth energies seems too much another expression of human arrogance, of anthro-pocentricity – though that feeling may in turn express my own greater love for the earth than for humanity.

Every aspect of nature is sacred. It is because we don't treat it as such that Druidcraft focuses on how to remember and express that absolute sanctity. Learning how to place our feet securely upon the ground, how to touch with nerves and soul awake, we develop our understanding of what *sacred* truly means.

The creation of altars and temples is another place to begin developing our focus. The beauty of Druidry is that a temple needs no roof or walls, an altar needs no finery; both are no more than guides that help us to focus. They encourage us to draw our minds into one moment in time and space, directing us to dedicate that moment to the intention of renewing sanctity.

In spending time creating or tending a temple or altar we are dedicating time to ourselves, giving ourselves a precious gift. This can feel like an act of selfishness, less valid than directly giving to others. Yet we know, too, that without making time for our own nourishment, we can become depleted. We need the inspiration gained that allows us to shine with our own spirit energy.

It isn't a complicated thing. An altar may be no more than a stone. A hearth can be an altar to the powers of fire, transformation and the beauty of home. A mantelpiece cluttered with photographs and memorabilia can be an altar to our ancestors, a candle lit in their honour. It is our intention that takes an object and, acknowledging it as sacred, accepting its life energy flowing through its own purpose, establishes it as an altar, as an expression and a reminder of sanctity.

I nag my students to spend time at their altars, to sit every day in quiet and simply be. It actually makes me smile when the word is misspelt in a journal or letter, written *alter* instead of *altar*, for the act does affect change. Committing to that time, whether five minutes or two hours a day, *alters* how we see the world, and so who we are. If we tack it into a daily routine so that our subconscious – body and mind – comes to expect it, anticipating and preparing for the focus, the benefit increases further, for our subconscious remains open to understanding and growing, to touch more deeply and be touched, to listen and truly hear, to see spirit and respond with perfect reverence.

We can make tiny natural altars: a few stones and a feather, a picture and a candle, a bowl of dried berries, leaves and fossil wood, a few shells and sea salt, a little collection of items that have inspired us to see again the richness of spirit. We could set a stone outside beneath a favourite tree, leaving upon it offerings for wildlife, gifts of our own creativity that will be happily devoured or dissolve back into the earth. Even a piece of wood, inscribed with its *ogham* (the early medieval Irish tree alphabet) may be enough, the mnemonic value of those magical letters reminding us not only of the spirit of that tree but of all nature and its wisdom.

We can also make complicated altars using carved tables and filling them with all the beautiful things we have ever found. We can lay out our chalice, blades, wands, semiprecious stones and symbols of this and that. It is important to remember, however, that none of this is necessary. An altar is a point of focus, set with beauty to turn our thoughts to beauty. It must not be distracting. When things become covered in dust, we might question their usefulness, perhaps returning them into the flow of life, passing them on, giving them away. Altars are best kept fresh and alive; even if the flow of nature that is honoured is that of decay, the space hung with spiders' webs and old leaves, there is a difference between an altar that is humming with energy and one that is simply not sufficiently tended.

A temple is not just a space within which an altar might sit, but in many ways it is an altar within which *we* can sit. Although at times I might want to climb onto my altar table and curl up by the candle and bones, washed by the scent of herbs, the cat inside me rising up to the surface, my human self knows that my cat self would cause chaos. The temple addresses this craving to be utterly within the high energy of the consecrated, for it embraces us, encircling all that we are.

In Druidry, a temple is always a temple to life, its tides and cycles. Created of or adorned with only that which inspires, a temple holds us safe from the distractions that tempt the mind into anxiety. Carrying us through the moments we give to it, a temple is a sanctuary, set at a distance from the world that wears us down.

Into its sacred space we can bring the crises of life, and there surrounded by what it's easier for us to see as sacred, as spirit and beautiful, the temple offers us the strength we need in order that we might honourably deal with the rest.

Temples can be entirely created by the natural world. Just as an altar may be no more than a mushroom-blessed tree stump, a temple might be something we stumble upon, a place vibrant with spirit.

Sometimes we come across places that appear simply to have evolved of the spirits' celebration of themselves, powers of nature flowing into a beauty that exquisitely touches our human perception. A natural grove of old yews in the midst of the forest, a dip on the moors where an old hawthorn grows, the enclosing curve of a living fallen willow by the water's edge, a great stone on a hillside that looks over the whole valley, the soft coolness of the cavern behind a waterfall – these places can be beyond the meanderings of humankind.

In built-up areas, too, we find natural temples, places made by human hands but for some other purpose; the obvious might be in parklands, whether an open ridge that overlooks the cityscape beyond, or a dark glade hidden by evergreens, holly and ivy. There are nooks and ledges to be found by rivers and canals, and havens of serenity in stretches of city graveyards. Flat rooftops are glorious sanctuaries of unexpected calm in the midst of urban distraction. For some people the most poignant temples are the art galleries, football games and wild clubs in which we dance, our souls completely focused on the colours and rhythms of passionate life.

Each one of these is intrinsically focused on different flows of natural energy: the powers of wind and skies, forest and growth, water, death, earth and even human nature. As seekers within a Pagan tradition, we do not use one temple or one altar to encompass the entirety of nature. Instead we pour our attention and reverence into different aspects at different times, different places and in different ways, so allowing ourselves the time and focus to build an understanding with each, intensely and effectively. As a result, a Druid may be connected to a number of temples. She may have many altars to life, but usually there are only a few that she tends frequently at any given time, those whose energy supports and guides her through the specifics of her *here and now*.

Fundamentally, what makes a Druid temple is what also makes the Druid's altar: it is simply the clarity of our intention. When we find a place that gives us the opportunity to sit undisturbed in reverence and reverie, a place that naturally and easily inspires us, the next step is to acknowledge it as such. We sit with the spirits of that place, waiting, listening, watching, gently building a connection sufficient for us to know whether our presence will be accepted.

A natural temple like this might need nothing altered. Indeed, it might strongly object to any little thing being disturbed. However, there are places that seem to reach out to us as we open ourselves to them, and a gentle process transpires, spirits eager or able to adapt, adjusting, listening, that together we can enrich and develop the beauty of that special place, sharing creativity. Moving a decaying branch will disturb the insects and fungi living on or beneath it, but it may be feasible if done with clear respect. Adding sacred objects – a bowl, blade, vase or figurine – may contribute a deeper or broader level of devotion to the temple, or it may be simply clutter.

Sometimes, in celebration or to focus aspects of our lives, we create our temples ourselves. These temples can be exquisite expressions of our own spiritual creativity, the vivid result of all that has inspired us. As delicious havens of sanctity, they are places into which we creep to breathe deeply, to sleep or dance in the arms of our gods. If we can't allocate a specific room or building, we can still honour and celebrate the flows of nature that pour through our hearth and home in the way that we decorate or set out our living space, in the area where we explore our creativity, where we study, work, play or make our food. A compost heap in the garden provides the focus for a wonderful temple, guiding us to honour the sacred in nature's powers of decay. By writing prayers on the door frame or using candles, we can create a temple of our bedroom in honour of home, love and family, sexuality and passion. An altar in the kitchen with an offering bowl for thanksgivings to the earth or our ancestors could be extended to make the kitchen itself a temple, honouring the source and flow of energy and nourishment as food.

There are times and places, too, where we need to create our own temples, places where the natural resources that might inspire us are thin at best or even absent, where without some effort we find it hard or impossible to see beauty, where distractions are chaotic, screaming for attention. Instead of giving up to the desolation of life, confused and uninspired, or turning from a place in disgust or resignation, the Druid commits to creating her temple, a shrine to life in all its tides and cycles.

In many ways, temples built in the worst places are the most powerful and the most important, for they remind us just where we need to work on our vision of spirit and *sacred*, motivating us to create beauty in places where before we saw only ugliness. Making a temple that overlooks a coal-fired power station, landfill site or military airbase may seem crazy and hard, but there are times when to do so is the only way in which we can truly understand how we might walk a path with honour in a world where such things exist; such temples don't honour the mess but allow us better to see our part in their existence and, taking responsibility, to find the sacred life energy that lays the path beyond their perpetuation.

Working with the spirits of place, our temple might be as temporary as our presence. I was taught that a Druid should walk away from a site after her ritual, leaving nothing behind her but the traces of her stories in the wind. It is a tenet that is not always easy to keep to, but it registers the difficulties of temples such as Neolithic stone circles, about which there are constant political arguments and upsets. To create a temple with nothing but intention, scattering song into the moonlight, and leaving like an owl on silent wings, most often feels to me the only honourable way.

In part this is the nature and purpose of 'casting a circle'.

Without walls to our temple, we delineate the edge ourselves. We could do it with ribbons, ivy strands, leaves, petals, nuts, shells or stones, or by pushing a toe into the sand or mud, making a little dip and ridge, thus marking the circumference physically in a way that will quickly disappear, decaying, being eaten, blown away in the wind, washed over by the tide. Some traditions call for casting in salt, but as salt kills, to do this would be anathema to Druid philosophy. On most occasions no *physical* marking of the boundary is needed; intention and magical flow are enough.

The reason why we use a circle is to reflect the cycles and circles of the natural world: a beautiful Amerindian expression speaks of the birds making their nests in circles because 'their religion is the same as ours'. In particular, we affirm the notion common in Indo-European and pagan spirituality that there is no beginning and no end, no moment of divine creation and no apocalyptic end in judgement. The ebbing and flowing process of emergence and dissipation, change and evolution, is perpetual and infinite, sometimes gentle and then dramatic, but never extinguished.

In reality, the circle of our temple does not need to be perfectly round, for adapting to the environment and moving in time temples often slide into the cornerless ovals that are common in nature. However elliptic it is poignantly different from the rows and pews of most strands of Christianity. When people gather together in the tradition, with the earth beneath them and the open skies above, the circle ensures that everyone is equally involved in the ritual, with no one standing above the others holding a rank of authority. Every person in the circle is accepted as bringing their unique gifts into that one place, that one *here and now*.

Even if we are alone, not needing to define a holding or guiding boundary around those gathered with us, it can be useful to create a temple for ourselves, encircling all we are and what we are about to do — whether that is a powerfully transformative ritual, working on our ability to touch and be touched, giving thanks and celebrating, or divinely blessed sleeping. By delineating the limits of our temple, we create an edge that holds us, giving us perhaps more confidence than otherwise we might have.

Of course, casting a circle can be a futile dance. We might read what it says in a book and follow it, letter for letter, or hear some teacher describe what should be done and attempt to copy this. Any dogma – for instance that the circle must be cast with a consecrated wand, that it is the scribing of a impenetrable line of silver-blue energy, that it must be cast clockwise starting in the east – is best respectfully ignored. Just as when we create our altars and temples of leaves, grass, music, silence, flowers, bones, mud, stone, concrete, moonlight or neon light, the casting of a circle is about our own unique expression of spirituality, sanctuary and sanctity.

If we know why we are doing it and we are sensitive to the energy, with a little guidance or affirmation we can find our own way.

━━◆━━

*Dusk, around four in the afternoon, and the crows are beginning to gather, circling above the leafless canopy, gossiping and chattering as they fly wing to wing high above me, sharing the stories of their day. From where I sit on the forest floor I watch as unhurriedly they land, settling here and there in the bare roosting trees. A couple of rooks break into a bickering,* rak-rak rak-rak-rak, *ending with an amicable* raah-craaa, *yeah well, nudging and shoving each other along the wide oak branch. Others are making that mutually comforting* krrr, *shaking out their feathers and sitting down on their feet.*

*My attention is brought back to ground by the barking of a stag, and I find that I'm smiling. He isn't far from me though I can't see him – a few hundred yards away I'd imagine – and his sharp call for his does' attention has brought me back to myself. I sigh and stumble to my feet, rubbing the aching in my legs as I try not to keel over.*

*'Oh sod it,' I murmur. I have sat still for too long again and, too cold now and too sore to stand, I slide back down to the mud and onto my knees. There I bend forwards, resting my forehead on*

my gloved hands now flat on the ground. My lady, I sigh again, this time exhaling and releasing the muscles of my chilled-tight body, let me feel your presence, I ask you. And soon enough the warm earth-blood energy is shimmering around me. Consciously and against my shivering instinct, I relax, opening myself, trusting the ethereal clay-red warmth that now silently seeps into my body and soul.

This time I manage to pull myself to my feet, my lady, thank you, and I turn towards the old oak, aware of the faint, clumsy crunch of my boots on damp fallen leaves. My words are those I've said so many times before as I reach for acceptance from this sleepy great tree spirit, and I feel the same response: the subtle energy of the oak spreads out from the bark to embrace me, holding me.

I close my eyes and steady my mind, softly speaking the clarity of my intention, fine-tuning with this tool of words the purpose for my quest, why I am here in the forest with night fast falling. Then, with gestures that are now such an integral part of the prayer to me, I make my call for peace, affirming my desire to listen without judgement, to do this work undisturbed and without myself disturbing anyone.

A breeze moves through the trees and I feel again the oak's energy. Within it I again let my stiff legs bend and, crouching, my hands once more on the cold mud and leaf mould, I call to my goddess of darkness. My mind spins, stretching, diving, out into the universe, the edgeless dark of the night skies, and the further I go the closer she comes to me, filling my lungs, my pores, every cell, until I break through into the inner dark of the atoms of the air I breathe, and I so crave release, wanting to let go and dissolve into the fullness of her power, but I hold back with a long, deep breath, whispering my request. And she steps even closer.

For a moment I pause, for I'm about to walk sun-wise, casting my temple's edge, pushing the energy out in that clockwise spiral of expansion. No, for this work I need to journey deeply inside. I affirm my connection to the flows of spirit, to her darkness, and I make my first step left, then another, following on, holding the

*intention undiluted, watching the trail of energy slipping from my*
*outstretched fingers. The blend is exquisite, a dark silver winter-*
*green of oak touching the richness of infinite black, the oak lining*
*the void of darkness that is slowly and so effectively separating me*
*from the world beyond.*

*I tie a knot at the place where I began, sweeping my intention*
*into a sphere of being, acutely aware now of this inner place I*
*have travelled to and of the distance it is from the forest outside.*

---

I have written elsewhere about the art of ritual, describing it as the ability to step from the fast lane of life's speeding highway onto the grass verge, temporarily taking a moment out of the current that propels us through time and space, and there remembering that life is sacred. I have spoken here of a temple as the environment that guides us towards that goal, and of the altar as being a focus. If being within the temple, sitting at the altar, we are still not freely able to reach that serenity and perfect vision, ritual is an effective tool to help us get there.

In its simplest form, ritual is merely the process of carefully creating and describing the temple around us.

We might literally do no more than acknowledge what we perceive in those moments. At times, there is nothing else that needs to be done; indeed, any other words or ideas would be redundant and distracting.

If we take more time to wake our vision, we can go further in our ritual, more fully acknowledging the location of the temple in both time and space, honouring the spirits that exist within that place, then stilling our mind with prayers for peace and harmony. Reaching out to cast our circle, we are finding and delineating the edges of our temple, using energies, colours and textures that feel easefully appropriate and so most congruously sacred.

We might acknowledge the floor of the temple, finding our feet upon the earth, mud, sand or grass; we might honour, too, all those who root and burrow in, or run and slide upon, that earth on which we stand. We can look up to our temple's roof, opening out to the skies, honouring the flying creatures on silky wings and feathers, the wind's dance, the clouds, the sun and stars reaching into darkest space. We might stretch out to the seas, the water flowing through our lands, spring and streams, the mist and rain, the blood in our veins, honouring all those who thrive within those worlds, too, or simply hold the dampness of the air, bowing to clouds thick with rain. In Druid parlance we call these the spirits of the Three Worlds, of earth, sea and sky, or the *spirits of place*, those of the environment immediately around us, and a ritual in their honour is powerful indeed. Every aspect of the temple that is relevant to our need is pointed out in words of poetry, prayer and poignance. We are honouring each spirit that inspires, each flow of creativity.

It need not be complex. Don't get stuck on the concept: it need be no more than one word placed after another, spoken with sincerity, honestly, as we acknowledge life and our environment with genuine respect. Too easily ritual can become silly theatricals without a good script.

Of course, a clear structure of ritual, a framework to follow, can be of profound value when we are learning the tradition, particularly while our ability to concentrate is less than useful. Without clarity of form, ritual can also readily degenerate into vague meanderings lacking direction. We might use others' words or ideas for a while, striving to understand and so express ourselves with depth, truth and integrity. However, as we find the ritual dance of our own body, we come to realize that the most poignant words we can use are our own. We are seeking relationship with the spirits around us, and any relationship will be distorted until we stand in our own shoes and talk our own truth.

The importance of speaking aloud can't be dismissed either. I say the *dance* of ritual, too, and by that I mean our physical movement. To make ritual in our imagination, to sit in stillness and quiet, letting our mind do the work of perceiving spirit and giving reverence, can have some usefulness – but the action too easily remains in the mind. Druidry is not about isolating ourselves in inner visions; it teaches us relationship, interaction and involvement. When we speak aloud, moving our body, our life energy flows from fingers to toes, through our brain and veins, affecting all that we are in our subconscious, in our bones. Only when the energy of our life-spirit is moving can we touch and be touched, better sensing and responding to the spirits around us.

Using our own voice, we might speak in Classical poetry or clumsy street talk, we might dance the moments alive with elegance and cat poise, walk in big boots and stand as strong as a bear, or move like an owl with as few words, changing utterly within – if we are being true to ourselves, it will work.

That we begin by finding focus says a great deal about the nature of Druidic practice.

As our perception gets sharper, we step closer to the vision of the Druid. Where before we were pushed and shoved by racing tides of distraction, anxiety and confusion, the tradition guides us to pause, settling into moments of stillness, *here and now*. Without needing to teach directly and assertively, its lessons of presence wake us to the sacred, both in the world and in ourselves. Through the Druid's lens the currents of life are revealed, and the powers and patterns of nature that underlie those currents. Inspired, we find connection, touching and being touched deep within.

Yet the path of any spirituality is not easy. Even if we have clearly made the choice to live, fully and with honour, stepping onto a dedicated path, along the way our commitment is challenged, sometimes subtly, sometimes with surprising brutality. Not just once, but again and again, we must make that active choice, affirming our motivation, if we are to find the strength to walk it.

Integrity, however, is not measured by knowledge but by intention, and once again this is honed by our developing focus. With each ritual performed, honouring the spirits of earth, sea and sky, we work on our ability to perceive clearly, our temples, altars, and circles guiding our vision further still. Cleaning the dust off our senses, beginning with touch, also aids the process, waking us to the vital essence of life that is so sacred.

We may accept that Druidry teaches us freedom, yet awake, present and committed to honesty, the path ahead can be daunting. There are pocketfuls of technique, tricks and tools that ease the journey, helping us beyond distraction, whetting our focus, finding stillness, and some of them I will describe in these pages. However, if we are truly to understand the nature of Druidry, not one of these tools must be considered vital. While we use them to learn, in the end what may be needed is for us to empty our pockets completely. Until that point, we step carefully, using every offer of guidance.

Increasing our awareness, focus tightens our mental discipline. Over time, as the numbness of habit and denial fall away, we can't help but discern more clearly who we truly are, becoming more alert to the patterns within our own human nature. Sometimes with gentleness, sometimes with a painful grip, we are held firm by the assurance of our growing honesty: if we are being true to ourselves, that truth exists both as stability underfoot and a magical touchstone for our direction.

With better focus, we turn to understand ourselves.

# Chapter Three

# Finding Oneself:
# Perfect individuality

Having found our feet, instead of heading off at a run, we hold the stillness for a while longer, allowing us to consider more deeply who and where we are. Fully awake now to the power of touch, along our journey of discovery it is scent that next commands our attention.

———◦———

*A calm afternoon, there's nothing to do. The book, lying unopened on my chest, rises and falls with my breath. I close my eyes, but only for a moment, for there it is again, now stronger than before, as if someone had held something briefly under my nose. I breathe in deeply, looking around, trying desperately to reach a box of memory files stored at the back of my subconscious.*

*I sit up. Papa? He's five thousand miles away yet I can feel*

*his heart pounding, a rush of anxiety. I dissolve from my*
*bedroom, reaching for him,* Are you OK? *He's not aware of me*
*and can't hear me, his soul completely directed elsewhere, but still*
*I feel him with me as if in some way he is calling for strength.*
*Back on my bed, again aware of the scent, I put my hand over*
*my heart and empathetically work to still his nerves, breathing*
*deeply until I feel him calming.*

*I lift my tea, wondering. The moist aroma of each of the herbs*
*steeping – yarrow, elderflower, catmint, thyme – swirling around*
*and through me, is very different from the musty sweetness that*
*came with my father. I close my eyes again, letting my mind slide*
*into the ethereal scent, silently, slowly, as if slipping into water.*

*Then I remember: patchouli oil. It's the cheap 'perfume' that*
*came with a doll I was given as a child in Spain. I'd scribbled on*
*its face, eventually pulling off its pink plastic head, wholly*
*unnerved by its fixed expression of stupefied delight: cheap and*
*dusty patchouli. I jump up and check the time.*

⋙◆⋘

When I spoke to my father, I discovered that at the moment I'd felt
him with me he was in the midst of a political rally perhaps two-
million strong. It was in the chaos of Venezuela's national strike,
and at the previous one he'd been tear-gassed, snipers firing live
rounds into the crowd; his anxiety was real, and as he gathered his
strength he'd reached for me subconsciously. At that moment, there
were women all around him, and that cheap Latin perfume I knew
so well had drifted through my father's breath and into my own.
I'd been woken by the scent of the exuberance of the crowd,
dressed in their nation's flags, dancing the passion of their anger,
sweat, dust and fear.

Smell, after touch, is our most primitive sense. We process scent
input in the oldest parts of our brains, where in evolutionary terms
we are still primeval furballs scampering from under the feet of the
dinosaurs. Fused with taste, it is the most evocative of our senses,
provoking fear, hunger, lust, curiosity, revulsion. Whether utterly

present or in past memory, it acutely places us in a moment. Even though we might mistake the smell, misidentifying its source and responding inappropriately, even with aromas that are broad or deep with many qualities, scent is always distinct, provocative, directive. Reaching for words to describe a smell or taste, we talk of pitch, note or tone, clarifying the sharp and the soft; we even speak of its resonance. In Druidry, these are words that we use to talk of spirit.

*Spirit* is the energy of life. By using the word, however, we are stating a perspective: that energy is sacred and worthy of respect. Yet it is just energy. It does nothing, goes nowhere. It isn't life, but the energy that allows life to be.

When the word refers to a specific creature, person or force, we are referring to the life energy held within that entity, the cohesive form of that individual. In ritual, in prayers or theological discussion, we might, for example, speak of the spirit of the forest, the spirits of the skies, the spirit of an ancestor: in doing so, we are referring to the energy of its essence.

That essence hums. As energy, it has a particular vibration: its note or tone.

I use the word *life* in a pagan sense, too; it doesn't only describe what conventionally we understand life to be, but holds within it the recognition that what science currently defines as 'life' is limited by what it can measure as such. A more accurate word might be *existence*, allowing within its definition an acceptance of life beyond current scientific parameters. We use *life*, however, for the word is rich with the poetry and connotations of feeling, flowing, being: experience. Life is the journey of the *soul*.

*Soul* is another word that needs definition, for it is used in so many different ways in different theologies and philosophies. One of the most common is the idea that the soul is the container of our consciousness or mind, and this touches the definition I use in Druidry. Understanding spirit as simply energy, the *soul* is that energy with intention: it has tumbled into motion.

Nothing supernatural propels the energy into motion. In Pagan Druid theology there is no creator whose craving for reflection caused the universe to come into being. Any stories of creation are recent inventions, expressing other influences. Instead, the greater mystery of existence is that it has always been here – as life emerging and receding, energy eternally flowing in currents, tides that wash forwards and fall back. Even the 'big bang' is perceived to be just one level of tidal movement within the eternal flow of existence.

Flowing through time, the soul moves from A to B, from germination to fruition, from birth to death, from the bus stop to the front door. It surges along a course of intention, a purpose of being. The level or character of its consciousness may be far beyond our ability to comprehend or perceive, and to talk of its desire or purpose may be misleading. In Druidry, the soul's drive is not some law of causality and retribution (like a poor Western interpretation of Hindu *karma*), nor a divine higher vision, destiny or fate; most fundamentally it is simply an expression of its own nature. Where spirit energy is held cohesively in one form, one moment and location, emerging through that cohesion comes a tide of purpose and identity. We might call it intention, the nature of its being, but more colloquially, and with a smile, I use the term *ishness*.

Going back to the idea of the forest, the essential energy that infuses it is spirit, but what makes it a forest and not a herd of buffalo is its soul, its forest nature that craves expression as forest-ness. In the same way, our spirit is the energy that shimmers within us, and our soul the current of that energy, moving according to our own human *ishness*, expressing the nature of our individuality as self.

Within this understanding, the physical world is the creativity of the soul. Upon its journey, the soul leaves footprints in time and space. Using the resources within its reach, our soul creates our body of flesh and blood, as does the tree create sap, bark, leaves and fruits. These footprints, traces of thoughts and intentions, are poignantly temporary. They remain for a while, then fade: all creativity is mortal, tidally emerging and disappearing. A powerful effect of such a perspective is an acceptance of death, of transience and change. We may love what we have made but we let it go, because our spiritual focus is not upon the creator nor creation, but on the vibrance and vitality of perpetual *creating*.

The spirit, like a scent or taste, hums at a certain pitch, but through the tides of its creativity this note shifts through the soul's journey of life. It changes not only with the soul's evolution, but also with the immediacy of its interactions, notes finding harmony and cacophony with others. As notes flow, streaming through, around and over each other, note following note, the soul composes the music of its life, the melodies of relationship, of growth and experience.

So do we speak of the soul's unique *song*. Whether it is the soul of a tree, a cat, a valley, a human being, a breeze or a waterfall, the soul is expressing the richness not only of its presence, but also of its history of memories and dreams. At any time its song tells of all it has been; in its creativity moments are held, a handful of notes captured like a bubble that – for a while – drifts, filled with memory, before bursting, disappearing. For those who can hear it and are attuned to the music of the soul, the notes played can naturally imply notes that are to come. So does the song also tell of the future.

Of course, while a waterfall or butterfly, each with a different kind of consciousness, might express its song with openness, the sticky complexities of human self-awareness mean that many people detest their own soul song. They try to hide it, suppressing their soul and all traces of its journey, its creativity, or they try to adjust it artificially, expressing notes that sound forced or empty.

Learning to accept our own song is an important part of the Druidcraft path. We find ways of facing our past, the discordance and crashing cymbals, the tuneless clatter and tiny cheap melodies. We learn to hear better how we are reacting to others' songs, holding the integrity of our notes instead of being thrown across random chords. Accepting others, we come to understand better just who we are, with all our cravings for escapism, drama, violence, denial and change. We discover ways in which we can stand up and yell aloud our soul song, however badly we might sing, confident in the truth that it is our own. We find our own voice.

Our journey of acceptance is also the process of expressing the song of the wild soul within us. Many twists in our life path may have shocked or wounded us into hiding our individuality and its creativity, but our wildness isn't simply the idiosyncratic side of who we are. The wild nature is that part of us which, through fear or conditioning, we believe is not necessarily socially acceptable. The culture we live in may be unambiguous, flinching from that which is not expected, predictable or conventional. The wildness is who we are once we have climbed out of society's catalogued box marked *SAFE*.

There is a cliché about Pagan religion defined as naked mud-splattered women in the midst of the forest, dancing uninhibited around a fire. Some of those who participate in Western Pagan practices shy away from the possibility, denying its existence as nothing more than media fantasy. Yet such wild expression is an important practice in Pagan Druidry, and for a number of reasons. In terms of deep reverence, being naked allows us to feel more acutely the relationship with the breeze, the wind, the skies, the light and dark, the ground beneath us, the warmth of the sun or flames, the touch of snowflakes or raindrops, the fullness of the natural world, and so encourages a richer, more genuinely felt interaction. Nakedness can also provoke or intensify the falling away of more than physical barriers, evoking an holistic vulnerability, a tangible soul honesty, not only in terms of how we relate to those around us – trees, rocks, moonlight, people, rain – but also with ourselves. Clothes allow us to hide truth, even from ourselves.

Of course, nakedness is not obligatory, nor is mud and screaming madness. But being true to ourselves is crucial, and if we are to find the freedom of that truth inhibitions must be discarded. Pretending to be 'normal' for fear of being rejected, alienated and isolated is counter to the tenet of revering nature and honouring life.

No one is actually 'normal'. Yet there are many people within mainstream culture who hold tightly to a concept of *normality*, basing it on what they feel to be socially expected and acceptable. Indeed, although this attitude is slowly changing, much mystical Druidic or shamanic experience is considered proof in Western culture of mental instability. I've worked with a number of people and heard of countless more whose 'illness' can be traced back, through the perverting and suppressing influence of psychiatric drugs, to lives that were perfect examples of eleventh per cent perception. Without the language of ritual, a spiritual framework or clear ancestral heritage to support them, the experience is too much to bear; the person is convinced that they are insane, and allows both the vision and others' fear of their vision to overwhelm them.

For those of us whose soul song is most often going to sound like Metallica at an Abba tribute concert, affirmation about the music of other wild souls is always a profound blessing. A constant flow of letters arrives in my in-tray from people talking of their deep perception of life, who are concerned as to whether or not I'll consider them insane too. They speak of sensing a dead relative, hearing the voice of a guiding spirit, laughter in the trees, music in the breeze, and seeing energy or dancing lights. They talk of longing to dance in the wind, to be naked in the rain, to howl with grief for no apparent reason. Many talk of powerful moments of prophetic vision, synchronicities of intuitive knowing. A smaller number speak more quietly of clearly perceiving the dead, of losing time in trance and more esoteric mysteries. To have a language that can explain or simply embrace these experiences and cravings is essential if we are to gain or retain any confidence of self-expression.

Every one of us has a streak of wildness in our soul, a part of who we are that wants to break away from the ordered world of human society. We need not be on the edge of madness to feel frustrated to the point of depression, but the feeling of being suppressed can drag us to the point of self-destruction. What could otherwise have been naturally creative can be explosive or implosive expression, a beautiful song shrieked under the pressure of distortion.

It could be said that psychiatry and psychology, and their various tributaries in psychotherapy, which fervently hold to their standard views of 'normality', have been more damaging to Paganism than any monotheism over the past century. They are an insipidly growing secular force in Western culture; like any other circumscribed religion with clear beliefs that holds its adherents together, their tenets inspire a fear of being lost in the wilderness of rejection – the seeker must meekly find his way back to being an accepting part of society, and acceptable to the whole. Although there are individuals in the profession who are exceptional healers and carers, and many who don't ascribe to the Judeo-Christian single supreme force that judges the good from the bad, God is too often simply replaced by the all-powerful Ego. Devoted to the self, the focus is utterly subjective.

Where a Druid will perceive the spirit or soul of another human being (whether alive or dead), a tree, a cat, a stream or stone, a psychologist construes delusion evoked by a fear of separation. Where a person feels nourishment from a forest, from solitude, or sees the fairies in the garden, or chats with spirits or a dead loved one, this is categorized as psychosis, an aberration to move through and leave behind. Quirks are acceptable in small, packaged doses, if held within the safety of a broader picture, but the individual is only healed when he once again knows how to adjust and place his individuality gently into the patterns of social convention.

Much of this psycho-babble of acceptability has also flowed into New Age healing and spirituality, reaching as these practices do for the gentle light, the one truth, the all-knowing universal divine being that is perfect love. Healing becomes a compulsion without which there is the horror of being less than flawless, shining with goodness and wholeness. Once again, the selfish focus is draped in a sweet smile, the guise of altruism and hyper-positive intent.

Druidry's regard for individuality is very different. Respecting the uniqueness of every bloodline, acknowledging the landscape's influence on every soul, it is expected that every person will be strange, inimitable, idiosyncratic. Each soul's eccentricty, each wild note played aloud is cause for celebration of life itself.

Wisdom, knowledge, healing, empowerment, radiance: these are not our focus, yet they come as symptoms of our questing for inspiration, our rambling through both the light and the dark. The idiosyncrasies and scars of our soul are a part of what makes us who we are, richness of our character gained through experience, not flaws to erase. We look for healing only when our creativity is stalled or our freedom of expression is hindered, not because we have to stand up straight in the line.

The sense of belonging found in Druidry naturally overcomes the human crises of isolation, dislocation and separation. It is an inevitable result of finding sacred connection with the spirits of nature – trees, dragonflies, streams – rather than perceiving life as merely matter. Our love of the dark doesn't come through simply facing the fear; nor are we hiding beneath its blankets. We celebrate the darkness as a fundamental focus of mystery, as the greatest universal force of nature. Trailing after the light of knowing becomes poignantly irrelevant.

The Druid celebrates with the dead, not just sensing their presence but dancing with them with exuberance, feasting with them in ritual and daily life, always feeling the community of ancestors that are ever with us, guiding us, witnessing our lives. Druidry teaches us to *hear the voices* of those souls who guide us, the stories of our ancestors, the songs of the dead. It guides us to hear the music of the wind, the tales held within the stones, the wisdom of trees, encouraging us to make powerful relationships where conventional perception sees inanimate soulless objects or needy delusion. It nurtures our ability to leave our bodies, to journey in our imagination into lands of fantasy, to dissolve into eleventh percentile vision, to travel upon the ether with the soul energy of our discarnate mind. It encourages us to leave footprints of creativity that exquisitely reflect our own wild truth and perception, inspiring others with the lucidity of their honesty.

We learn that to judge another's reality as unreal is not just ignorant and narrow-minded; it is also dishonourable.

After touch, smell and taste, the next sense that we study in the tradition is hearing. I send my students off to spend long hours, months of daily practice, preferably in the spring time when the waking songs of re-emergence are so vibrant after winter's quiet.

At first they are impatient with the frustrated irritation of not quite understanding, but slowly the paradigm shifts. They come to realize just what it is to hear fully.

Physically, we can use our ears to hear, yet our ears are simply vibration collectors wired to our brains to dispense acute responses. In fact, our whole body picks up sound, waves of energy vibrating. Standing close to a foghorn or the woofers at some gothic-industrial nightclub, it's easy enough to feel the oscillations of the bass sound pushing right through us. In Druidry we learn how to hear a wren's song with our fingertips.

We listen, too, to that which seems to make no noise, yet still hums with vibration: we *hear* the earth pulsing with our feet, the light of the moon with our neck and shoulders, the sharp-sweet greenest song of the apple with our eyelashes. We are hearing the spirit, the soul as it sings.

In the beginning, we simply wake the physical nerves to vibration, without any analysis, allowing no intellectual reason or reaction. Gently, once we have sufficient confidence in the experience, when our chattering scepticism and self-doubt can be surmounted, we can let ourselves think about what we hear. In time, adding our emotional faculty to the mix, we learn how sound vibration inspires or provokes us to feel, the soul song of a hungry kitten or a poplar in a warm breeze, the note of the sea as the sun sets into its horizon; we start to listen with our hearts.

Once we are conscious of our own spirit energy, and better able to perceive clearly the essence of another, the tradition then guides us to hear with our own soul, completely open to give and to receive, interacting spirit to spirit. From within the vibration of our own notes, our own spirit tone, we hear another's vibration. Brilliantly clear, it touches every cell of our being. Aware of notes overlapping notes, harmonies and harmonics, as we listen to the full moon we hear the lunar rock, the darkness, the sun's reflected light, the mist, the air's movement and we hear ourselves.

Yet our worlds are full of distractions. We create a good deal of them on purpose to fill our time with dross, with inconsequential worries. Learning to listen requires focus, a mind undisturbed.

Serenity doesn't come easily. It takes many years of dedication to achieve the state of inner peace and freedom that allows us truly to hear. One of the tools we use is what is often called meditation, yet in many ways Druid *meditation* is simply the craft of listening.

Unlike Eastern techniques (as often taught within Western culture), meditation is not a striving to put aside thoughts and sit with an empty mind. Meditation is about relationship, about being thoroughly engaged. It is a journey that begins with following our natural flickers of curiosity, for without curiosity there is no possibility of developing an honourable relationship. Once it is secured, we continue by going deeper, cultivating our interest until we are able to maintain attention, then extending that into concentration, until we are utterly involved, awake and open, spirit to spirit: this is meditation. It is a state that brings sublime calm, refuelling body and soul.

As an example that is possibly one of the easiest to try, our curiosity is often kindled by the colours of the setting sun. Sitting down to watch, the flow of interest deepens so that we become naturally yet fully attentive to each changing moment, concentrating on colours and cloud formations, losing any sense of ourselves as we open to the experience, immersed in our connection with the sun and our environment, listening to the songs. With the sea, a river, fire, stars or a dear friend, we can both deepen our relationship and develop our ability to hold ourselves undistracted. So does the Druid learn to meditate with a pebble, an apple, the whole valley, a single blossom, a sick child or the soul of a man long dead, moving through moments of perfect relationship, silent interaction, without any need to be or do anything but exist together, fully present, listening.

We think of the bards of the Druid tradition as those who sing the songs and tell the tales of our ancestors – the folk musicians and myth keepers. Yet, in the culture of our twenty-first century, the bards are also the novelists, the playwrights and screenwriters, the rock musicians and composers, the documentary makers, reporters, journalists, social columnists and political satirists, the stand-up comics of our time. They are now, just as they were two thousand years ago, the word-magicians and craftsmen of sound.

It is, of course, a crucial part of bardcraft to master the instrument that you use, whether that is the flute, the bass guitar or the breadth of your own voice. However, the power of the bard isn't sourced in this skill; we all know of musicians who are technically brilliant yet somehow don't move us with their music. The power is not in playing, singing or speaking, but in *listening*. So is the craft of the bard one that is integral to the Druid tradition; in fact, in most courses of Druid training, once the basics have been covered, even if he will not practise in this field of work, the student embarks on the long, tough training of the bard: LISTEN!

Whether the story is that of the goddess-heroine Rhiannon from the mythology of south-west Wales, or that of the death of a child in a religious community in north London, the bard can only retell the tale if he has truly heard it first, his soul open to every nuance and twist, every emotion implied and provoked.

He learns how to hear the soul song of all those involved, including that of the person who himself tells the tale. He learns not to mimic (although this is a bardic trick in itself), but to acknowledge and utilize his own song of experience in the process of hearing and retelling it again, the notes touching notes, creating harmonies and resonance, sounds that soothe or grate, comforting or waking.

The bard learns, too, how to create stories and music from the immediacy of relationship. Perched on a fallen tree in the midst of the forest, with her flute she learns to play the song she hears, of wind and leaves, mud, trees and squirrels. Sitting on the dusty ground in a city square, he finds the songs of the flow of humanity, the ground beneath, the trees, buildings and traffic, playing them through his clarinet. On stage, she listens to every lift and fall of breath in the auditorium, the hum of lights and the earth beneath, as she finds the words to captivate the audience before her. So is the bard present, responding to the *here and now*.

*She looks up, but her eyes see nothing of what is around her.
With every pore and muscle she is listening; the stillness as her
fingers lift momentarily from the harp strings is as rich with
sound as when she is in full voice to its music.*

*I reach forwards in spirit, stepping a little closer towards her,
craving an experience yet deeper, wanting more fully to submerge
into the music. She is more than playing; it's as if she is invoking
the sound that she is hearing from another world, drawing it so
carefully through ethereal cracks. I half open my eyes to see a little
more, my spirit dancing like a languid flame, curling, turning,
stretching around her, every cell shimmering with the vibration of
the strings, and for a brief moment I do see. Within her, beside
her, behind her, an old man plays, his smaller harp on his lap
while hers is set upon the floor. I can almost feel the tiniest delay
that is the gap between his rough growl of song and her allowing
the words to slip through her as, hearing his music, she fills the
room with life. It's like the taste of warm honey passed from
mouth to mouth in a sun-blessed kiss, the intimacy of the bond,
the teacher and student, the muse and musician, the tale passed
down through generations. And in that second, I glimpse, too, the
bard that sits within/behind him, and another within him, and
another, like mirrors mirroring mirrors, reflections stretching back
in kaleidoscopes of sound and time.*

*With the wonder of life shining in me, I step back, sitting
again in my body to watch from the audience as she plays. And
as the song comes to an end and the place is filled with the
crackling noise of applause, I find I am clapping, too, the old man
with the gravelly voice and the one who taught him the song, bard
before bard before bard through time. And she smiles as the
appreciation touches her, and in her smile is the integrity and
honesty which show that she drinks it in for all those who have
sung the song before.*

---

Not every voice we hear is beautiful, and not every word is wise
or caring, whether we are listening to the breeze, butterflies, the

traffic or the dead. Yet inspiration comes not just from the easy moments of life, and we are taught not only by those who love or respect us. Nor are the stories that must be retold often those that make us comfortable. So do we accept the need to hold the stories of our own blood and personal heritage.

When we talk within Druidry of honouring our ancestors, we don't mean those who lived in some era far enough away in time to be idealized and abstract. Honouring our ancestors begins with the acceptance of our parents, as loving or brutal as they may have been. It means holding no denial about the weakness and cruelty that has passed through our bloodline, as genes, as conditioning and patterns of behaviour.

Just as we can deeply root into the earth, interacting with the energies, finding nourishment and stability, so can our soul find its roots in time, through blood, genes and stories. Each blood root hums with strengths and flaws, with inherent talents, blind spots, creativity and destruction, the qualities that poignantly express our ancestors' lives, people whose journeys have helped create all that we are. Their songs resonate within us.

'Forgiveness' is not a word that I use in Druidry. Because I consider it way beyond the reach of humanity to forgive with sincerity, I can understand how other religious traditions ascribe it as a quality of supreme deity. My theology has no such god, though; while I consider it a human construct, I don't perceive forgiveness as a human characteristic. The word I do use, however, is one that is critically important in terms of honouring our ancestry: the word is *acceptance*. Druidry teaches us to accept.

When we are cut off from our blood roots, we are neither nourished nor held. We may feel safer, protected from the pain of our parents or their parents, but our opportunities for healing, for learning and growing, are compromised by the lack of connection. When we are able to find acceptance, the effect is extraordinary: a profound sense of stability within perpetual change, the power of evolving through continuity. Spirit flows like a river, life energy coursing through generations.

Listening to our ancestral songs, finding the notes of our genes, our history, blood and bones, the wash of continuity through evolution is exquisite, sometimes painful but always poignant. To sing those songs with our family can be a deeply healing, but even where this is not possible – through lack of accessibility or understanding – there is a resonance that can heal, provoking change, albeit without direct communication. The sound of the songs in our minds guides us, holding us firm upon our path.

Anything that facilitates honourable relationship, starting with acceptance, can be used to create an altar to our ancestors: photographs, a candle to light, jewellery or memorabilia, a vase of flowers. There might be symbols of what individuals of our bloodline have achieved, whether that is an engineering project or a recipe for the best ginger parkin in Shropshire. Like any altar, this one is a space dedicated to sacred interaction, created in order to remind us of what is truly important.

Honouring our ancestors is not altruistic, and we do not do it in order to gain points and raise our score with some judgemental god. We do it to achieve our own freedom responsibly claimed within the web of connection: in accepting the flaws and the achievements of our ancestors, we can better accept, understand and celebrate our own.

Even the smallest steps keep us moving forwards on the path, and each one can be taken with a breath touched with wonder.

Only once we have studied *earth* and established our roots more strongly, both in time and space, does it make sense to look up to the skies, to reach into the power and beauty of *air*. With a greater truth and certainty about all we have been, now can we extend up and out into the canopy of our souls, exploring all we can yet be.

The 'tree meditation' is almost a cliché in modern Druidry. Its appeal has spread into New Age healing, personal development, even business consultancy: it's an effective visualization, even when done with little training and minds half focused. The image of being balanced between earth and sky, solidly rooted and yet growing free in the wind, affords a poignant sense of self. Its power comes not least because the image is definitively whole, allowing a vision of self that is greater than human physicality yet still has form, clear edges, and the vibrancy and potential of breathing-growing life. It infuses us with confidence in terms of both stability and hope.

In Druidry the image of the tree-self also provides us with the foundation of an important concept: the *nemeton*. The word used to be understood as a sacred grove, a woodland temple of the ancient Druids, but this is a limited interpretation. More clearly, a nemeton is a sacred sanctuary, and such places are powerful in part because their boundaries are distinct.

The nemeton may be a physical temple, stone circle or forest grove, but more often, in this spiritual tradition where most people practise alone, it refers to a far more personal idea: it is the sacred haven of the individual. It is that place where we go in order to let go of the world, where it is easier to feel safe and free, to breathe in the beauty of the earth. It is our private temple, an expression of ourselves, our love and our need writ in a sacred manner, whether under the trees at the bottom of the garden, deep in some hidden valley, or even in the cupboard under the stairs.

Yet there is more still to this concept. For, perhaps most poignantly, we speak of the *soul nemeton*: the temple within which we live and breathe. That clichéd tree mediation is a sound tool here, for standing rooted into the earth, branches spreading out into the skies, our sense of self becomes more acute. It's an extended self, glorious with all we have been and can be, but as such the image is enhanced: from the tips of our branches to the tips of our roots, we find awareness of this our nemeton, the temple sanctuary of our body and soul.

Naturally, our spirit shines out around us. When we are strong, brilliant with our own life energy, the radiance extends out from the core of our being, glowing, shimmering. Letting go the image of the tree, it is this area into which we shine that defines our soul nemeton. It is naturally protective. Close around us, it is an area into which we would comfortably allow only those we trust utterly, with whom we have a close physical or emotional relationship. We also call it our *intimate space*. It expresses the undiluted truth of who we are.

In reality, however, we seldom have sufficient consciousness or confidence in that inner strength. Even when we do feel our spirit shine, our limits can feel indistinct and inadequate as protection. Instead, subconsciously, often irrationally, erratically, we learn to reinforce the edges of our soul nemeton, building up the barriers around our intimate space in unambiguous self-defence. Holding our truth, our raw, wild, honest intimate self, we know these edges are crucial and, whatever state they are in, for as long as we are able, we defend them fiercely, for it is within that space that we can be most brutally wounded. With true self-expression such a key within Druidcraft, it is no wonder the soul nemeton and its barriers are such an important issue.

The Craft teaches us first simply to become aware of our present state. It can be unpleasant to realize how tense or self-defending we are, how broken, blurred or scarred. Yet awareness guides us to understand better who we are, our presentation of who we are and just why our relationships are as they are.

Growing conscious of our nemeton is rather like learning how to wiggle our ears or flare our nostrils: it appears quite absurd until we find the knack. Even for those without eleventh per cent vision, it is often possible to sense the edge with fingertips or hands, feeling a slight pressure, a change in temperature or light in the air. Simply by using our mind, pure intention and openness, a blend of imagination and sensitive vision, we can trace the edge, not forgetting the area to either side and behind us. Scanning the edge like this, it is possible to perceive changes in colour and texture, areas that reveal weakness, tension or wounds. Where the edge is vague or tight, this is often reflecting a crisis in the physical body, energy flinched creating physiological stress, energy dissipated creating vulnerability. When a seer senses potential damage in the body, what she is perceiving is an area where the life energy and/or nemeton is taut or faint.

We might perceive the energy of the edge in colour, as a texture or substance. Some people use solid steel to secure their safety, or defensive razor wire, or walls of breeze block; others put up KEEP AWAY or DON'T TOUCH signs. Some do it with invisible perspex, appearing to be welcoming yet remaining aloof, thwarting contact, ever distant and inaccessible. Some have brittle edges that are easily broken, existing with sharp cracks in both their defensive walls and the integrity of their self-expression. Some paint their nemeton opaque, remaining enigmatic, incomprehensible.

Other people have no clear boundaries whatsoever; their sense of safety and individuality drift like a heavy dye in still water, always hopelessly vulnerable to illness and abuse, to the pushing and pulling of others' needs. For some, the nemeton has become so acutely flinched that it exists only within the physical body, a critical state of tense self-protection that allows abuse of the body to continue.

Where life grants the opportunity, we share our mother's sanctuary from not long after conception until we start to forge our own, fighting the boundaries and fears between the ages of eighteen months and three years. It is the mother's job then not only to release the child from her own sanctuary, but also to teach the child gently how to create his own. It's a difficult transition. Indeed, the connection to our parents remains, energy humming through an ethereal umbilicus, until once again we start to push, stumbling through adolescence to discover who we are and find our independence, and that cord at last transforms into a connection based on choice. Where that transition is not achieved, the bond becomes draining and destructive.

Accepting more fully who we are as individuals, with all the sludge and fog and grit of our minds, accepting our soul song and our nemeton, allows us to confront barriers to freedom and potential. Consciousness is usually enough to set into motion a process of change: the awareness of how we protect our intimate space sheds light on a great deal, and we can follow through with shifting attitudes and clear intent. Deep healing can be effected, too, through dance, stretching, massage and other kinds of body work, all of which can provoke cognizance, release and affirmation of strength.

The nemeton that is healthy shimmers with life in all the colours of our truth and experience. It is utterly flexible, a magical bubble. We flinch gently to protect ourselves when it is necessary to do so, relaxing easily once again when the threat has passed, either subconsciously or totally awake to what we are doing. Keenly aware of our edges, our natural boundaries acknowledged, we can explore that greater freedom of truth, honesty, potential creativity and presence.

An understanding of the nemeton is also a key to increasing the poignance of casting a circle as a Druid temple. Understanding that our nemeton is the natural protective boundary around our body and soul, whether emerging naturally through the radiance of our spirit energy, or created in order to hold that intimate space more secure, in casting a circle for ourself we can simply do so as an extension of our nemeton.

The value is evident: a wider sanctuary for the soul.

⋙━◆━⋘

*Too damp after the rain to be hard with frost, the earth is soft enough underfoot for me to walk with barely a sound, and with each footfall I let my energy sink down into the mud, the rhythm of my steps a prayer, both of and for acceptance. I can see nothing beneath the stiffness of my knees, nor more than a couple of feet before me, the darkness of the night consummate, thickened by cloud, untouched by moonlight. Yet as I walk I move through the energy of the trees, my own movement increasing the impression of theirs, tree spirits reaching towards me, spirit branches swaying through me. At times I can see more clearly when I close my eyes.*

*The presence of the beech touches me long before I reach her. There's no obsequiousness, but the smaller trees – the birch, the hazel, the elder and may – all acknowledge her broader higher energy, like pieces of different sizes in a jigsaw puzzle gently fitting together into one congruent picture. Acutely aware of my movement, I seek the puzzle pieces where I too can fit, stepping carefully with ease, utterly connected, edges sliding together.*

*At the fringe of the clearing I stop. A little more light here touches the forest floor, though not enough to perceive anything but the impression of shadows within the darkness. I sigh and breathe, feeling my spirit seep down into the mud, its clay-blood energy shimmering about my boots, rising up through my veins until I raise my arms, sighing once more as the sky mist falls over me, tasting my presence, sinking around me. And I smile with the strength that infuses my soul, feeling as wide as the valley, as tiny as a fleck of dust, my grandmother standing beside me, her tender spirit silence touching my heart.*

*And I step forwards, one step, to the edge of the tree's spirit. Not yet under the reach of her branches, my weight upon but the furthest of her roots stretching out beneath the ground, the change in the air before me is distinct.* Sacred spirit, *I whisper, almost aloud,* you know who I am ... once again I come here in peace, with the gentleness of my soul, my intention to honour the waking day, seeking inspiration ... *In the quiet before dawn, the first dreams of spring unfurling in the mud, she listens with frost clarity from deep within. Offering my own truth, my trust, I ask,* may I enter your temple? ...

*The acceptance is palpable. As I walk forwards into the clearing beneath her bare canopy, I am washed through with her song, like the certainty of real laughter and the scent of mist-wet wood. And with my body aching in the cold, for a long while I simply sit on the mud in the darkness, breathing.*

*When the first scents of dawn touch my breath, I open my eyes, and slowly struggle to my feet with all the clumsy rustling of my clothes. I affirm my balance, my connection with the spirits of earth and sky.*

*My nemeton is soft, held within the arms of the beech, open to her energy, but I must find more coherence in order to work. When I ask, she lifts me gently with her acceptance, and I reach deep within me for the darkness of my goddess.* My Lady, lend me your touch ... *as I scribe with my finger a circle beneath the grey canopy. Weaving its end to its beginning, I step back into the centre; I can see it in the air, a line that lies like a gap in time and space, encircling me. I close my eyes, sweeping it into a* sphere, above and below, then quietly breathe, with every breath softening further my soul's edges, letting myself spill out, as if my form were gently melting, dissolving into the air, filling the circle that lies around me.

The sense of freedom lifts my soul. Held utterly by the beech, I stretch the aching of my body within that bubble, set aside, cast with the innermost darkness of the void; I dance the pain of each limb, exploring the reach of every nerve. I feel unburdened. Though I am wrapped in half a dozen layers of clothes, I feel joyfully naked.

My grandmother smiles.

Come through me, I murmur, and she dissolves into the mist beyond my circle, emerging within my heart, my blood alive with her song, and together we dance, in my boots, jumpers, fleece, big coat, as light as thistledown on a hazy summer's afternoon. We find moments of tension and with soundless laughter push them over into free-fall, diving, gliding, spinning into freedom, and where pain shrieks, hand in hand, we chase it laughing, until it disappears into illusion.

How long we dance, I don't know. I never know. But the forest is changing, the sun close now to breaking the horizon across the valley, some spirits withdrawing, some only now waking. The last of the rooks are chattering before leaving their roosts, heading off over the meadows for a day of ease and exploration. I too have prayers to make, a few questions to ask in order to clarify the course of the day ahead. Into my hands I let fall the issue to deal with.

A high whistle strikes my circle, the energy trembling in response. Someone is out with a dog, creating havoc in the calm. I breathe to affirm my centre and call to the beech. In perfect gentleness she seems to smile. The edges of my cast-nemeton, chasms of black, transform silently into the greys of winter bark and the dull greens of last year's growth. I sit motionless within, breathing through beech roots.

A woman, wrapped up in scarves, a thick coat and scattered thoughts, strides down the path and on without noticing. The scruffy terrier at her heels stops to sniff the edges of the circle.

*Curious, he pauses, looks around confused, then scampers off after her down the path.*

———◆———

In my misspent youth, in the flush of learning magic when all kinds of tricks still worked a treat, before ethics and a broader vision limited my actions, I found I could camouflage my nemeton in the classroom, and was seldom challenged by the teacher or drawn from the novel I was reading beneath my desk. On a train, I cloaked myself with the coats and newspapers and thoughts of the passengers around me, and the ticket collector would pass me by. In a bar, hustled in the throng of the crowd, I would light my circle with neon, flashing emerald green, catching the attention of the barman ahead of my turn; I would pad my nemeton with raw electric energy so that anyone who came close would be needled with static, and people gave me space in a crush.

Although at times such tactics might be useful, needless to say they can also be selfish: unnecessarily bad behaviour. Understanding the way our souls work gives us options we didn't have before, and that power can be used equally positively or harmfully.

A crucial part of our Druid perspective is the honouring of others' intentions, of needs and truths. Of course, we can do this intellectually, recognizing their reality – if only through glimpses. Yet, when we can perceive and appreciate another soul's intimate space, their nemeton, the way we relate to that person changes accordingly and often radically. Simply accepting the soul sanctuary of another being – tree, stream, child, mountain, spider, lover, client, friend – whether or not we are able to perceive it distinctly physically or emotionally, we can no longer push unnecessarily, disrespectfully. We listen. For within the nemeton of every soul is the music of their history, the stories of their experience, the wholeness of who they are, in all their strengths and weakness. We can't help but hear the song, for its vibration touches us, life's energy humming through life's atoms, but *listening* is what we learn to do, that we may live with honour.

# Chapter Four

# Finding Connection:
# The web of awen

*Rays of the evening sunlight are glancing off the rippling of the lake. The* thuck *of a ball, the call of players, touches me from the basketball court nearby. A young lad races by on skates, his wheels spit-snarling on the gravel bumps of the path. A group chatters on the grass, but nothing moves the calm of my gaze. On a dead branch that reaches out from the island's haphazard growth sit four cormorants, their jet-black feathers smooth, their bodies hunched down upon their feet. And they too gaze, unmoving, as if the world all around them were a dream, the vitality of their day's diving holding them enchanted, like wordless memories of colour, laughter and love.*

*I turn to my colleague, a brief glance, affirmation, and we share a smile. There are so many things awaiting us, to be organized and discussed, decided upon and attended to, each issue fidgeting in its need for an immediate response. Yet here, on the park bench,*

*we sit side by side, watching the day coming to its close without*
*conversation. There is nothing that we need do that is more*
*important than this moment, sitting wholly together, our souls*
*affirmed with calm, like cormorants at sunset.*

———◆———

In our Western culture, both our society and our English language are weighted with bias towards an attitude of dualism: we jump to clarify opposites, opponents, left or right, needing the certainty of black or white, good or bad, in or out. Either with us or against us, there is no middle ground but that which provokes the threat of weakness and mistrust; our culture is always looking for its adversary, and at the source of this is the distinction between body and mind that is dualism. Physicality and spirit (here synonymous with soul or mind) in dualistic thought are considered to be made of discrete and dissimilar constituents. This is a Christian or monotheistic perspective, yet, like so many ideas embedded after centuries of religious dogma, this dualism underlies our culture as if it were a basic fact, standing broad in its pomposity with all its priorities, moralities and prejudices intact.

Because its perspective distinguishes between the vulgarity of physical matter and the intangible sacred spirit, where the latter is hard to perceive or understand or imagine, it is religious beliefs that fill in the gaps of comprehension. Yet, when we can't subscribe to those beliefs, denying a religion's authority of vision, few discard the complete dualistic concept, so entrenched is it in our culture; instead, while spirit is dismissed as an implausible religious concept, what is retained is the resigned acceptance of the mud and bones of basic matter. As a consequence, without fear of God or judgement in terms of current behaviour, or any sense of the sacred or divine within nature, the physical world in itself ceases to matter. In lives that are entirely finite, in an environment that is simply a resource, society becomes rapacious in its consumerism, taut with greed, hunger and paranoia.

During the plenary of a conference recently, at which I was a speaker, a Christian evangelist questioned the source of my morality; he was unable to conceive how Druidry could be ethically secure or acceptable without God. My response was to suggest that his question was a clear expression of his complete lack of experience in terms of the sanctity or divinity of nature; and this is where we find the Pagan Druid's vision as non-dualistic.

Natural or nature-based spirituality requires no belief in the supernatural. There are no religious concepts to accept or reject. The Druid speaks of spirit simply as life energy considered sacred; the soul is that energy flowing through time and space along a current of intention, an energy we might understand too to be the mind or psyche, rich with its visions, memories and dreams. These two are not separate from physicality, or integrally different in terms of essence, for matter emerges as a direct result of our soul's intention, energy slowing into tangible form as an expression of its creativity: as I have said before, the mud and bones are simply the soul's footprints in the sand, footprints that will dissolve with the next tide.

Furthermore, it is this understanding that offers the powerful foundation of Druid ethics, for the morality emerges naturally from the increasingly profound relationships that are forged between each individual and the spirits and forces of nature. Perceiving everything as sacred but essentially as just energy – not flesh, metal, bark, mud, held in separate physical packages – the way in which we touch and interact is seen as naturally deeper. We are all connected, all the time.

This connection, energy touching energy, spirit touching spirit, is referred to in the tradition by the analogy of a web. The threads that connect us are always there; what is needed is for us to wake to them, not as a theory, or an understanding or possibility, but as an holistic experience. We learn to *feel* and *live* through the inherent connections, accepting this vision of co-action and relationship, then mastering how we can open our souls in order to intensify the experience and grasp its ramifications.

For as our understanding develops and our bank of experience extends, so too does our sense of personal responsibility. Within the web, we come to realize ourselves to be crucially and perpetually affecting parts of an integral system: the ecology of our home, the environment and the planet. There is no force of authority beyond nature that will judge our action and so guide us into ethical behaviour; there is, instead, the exceptional quality of our own respect and devotion for nature's powerful currents, within and around us, intermingling and utterly connected.

Responsibility is an awkward word, passed on quickly by many as if it were a hot potato or a label of culpability. Yet if the word is broken into parts, it can be understood as a serene gift rather than a burden: the ability to respond. Within the web of spirit, without taking on blame or obligation inappropriately, being able to respond to a situation with relevance and honour is a potent skill, and one that can only be learned through dedicated practice. We learn responsibility as a freedom, a commitment to be ourselves, in perfect communication and self-expression, sourced in acceptance and honour. Here, too, the nemeton is a key.

Through our blood roots of ancestry, our mud roots of physical presence, together with our canopy of dreams and desires, as our awareness of our nemeton grows, so patterns and explanations emerge within the colours and textures of its edges. Even where our understanding is cracked, we can see just how we protect ourselves. The nature of our nemeton, and how we present ourselves to others, becomes clearer; the way we succeed or fail in relating to others becomes more obvious. We learn to know and to accept who we are.

The same is true for the world around us. Slowly, as we learn how to acknowledge others by their nemeton, so do we learn to accept who they are, and to respond consciously and appropriately as a result. For in the quality of the nemeton, we are perceiving the energy of the song in all its strengths and weaknesses, in all its truth.

In the natural world beyond humanity, where the neuroses of self-awareness don't occur, when a creature alters its nemeton the change is usually overtly reflected in the physical form (like a possum playing dead, or a fish colour blending with the sea floor). Some animals use tricks like those we learn in the Craft, or in martial and performance arts, holding back or pushing forwards, utilizing the energy and force of the nemeton's edges to hide or to command attention, appearing fiercer, more glorious or insignificant. Although we too can play such games, altering our edges to pretend to be something we are not, even when we are convinced we are successfully fooling the world, most of humanity sees straight through the guise. We may fall for lies, we may be too tired to look at all, but usually on some level we *feel* who someone truly is. The energy of their soul song touches us. Sharp or fluid, fluorescent or dark matt, brittle or flexible, our edges are fuelled by our spirit energy, and one way or another they express the stories of our souls.

We don't need to know why a soul is like it is – although to do so may ease the developing or deepening of a relationship. Yet only if we acknowledge and accept the song of another's nemeton will our interaction be responsible. Being upset by a person's incomprehensible aloofness, confused by a sudden aggressive reaction or frustrated by a persistently negative response: these all imply that we are interacting without respect for the nemeton of those involved. Whether heavily defending or erratic and cracked, the edges of another's sanctuary must be recognized. We need not like what we see, nor stick around, but we can still act with responsibility and honour.

Connecting consciously with another person on this level, nemeton to nemeton, is to meet in honesty. Our soul touches another soul, true intention encountering true intention. Where there is friction or lack of trust, that contact will be fleeting before natural repulsion or caution draws us apart, yet where the notes fit together the effects are poignant. The acceptance is powerful, the music washing through us as our song rises, influenced by the other. To share moments with someone in this way, playing together, is truly precious.

Although with energy touching energy, we might feel tremors both physically and emotionally, consciously connecting, nemeton to nemeton, need not be physical. Intimacy without body touching body is a powerful way of expressing our soul truth, for often physical nerve sensation can distract from deeper connection: a kiss, for example, can be an easy way of avoiding eye contact. The same is true using the language of spiritual intimacy.

A clear example I have used many times is the idea of the New Age enthusiast who has been led to understand that hugging trees is good for the soul, and yet has no sensitivity towards the tree itself. The image of the tree recoiling from the burly hugger, nemeton flinched, snarling, *Get this creature off me!* provokes laughter, but it is a serious notion. Instead of finding a tree and running up to the trunk to fling our arms about it, getting bark and beetles in our hair, if we were instead to stop at the edge of the tree's nemeton and ask, with clear and listening respect, if it would be possible to touch, soul to soul, the moment of connection would be far more powerful and moving, even if we were still twelve feet from the trunk.

So do we learn how to walk our journey with more respect, listening, watching, sensing, eliciting clearer interaction, evoking and expressing the surety of responsibility and truth.

———◆———

*She stands alone, shivering, albeit fully within the chatting group. Now and then, her arms will relax a little, the dark blue of her nemeton dropping like a length of heavy material around her. She is so thin, it seems almost more substantial than her physical body.*

*The young man speaks a little more loudly, his hand moving clumsily, with affection, to emphasize some point expressed, and the others laugh, their energy quivering with the dance of it, and though she smiles a little, appreciating some memory of laughter herself, as she does so she pulls the heavy blue cloth more closely about her. In her exhaustion she is incompetent with it, leaving great areas of herself uncovered, her persistent soul-nakedness only tiring her more deeply.*

*I am about to walk towards her, to help her to wrap her soul with my affirmations, hauling up the old material to hang it more securely about her shoulders, but a woman she knows makes it before me. I watch through the crowd as she touches her arm softly, letting her know she is there.*

*The woman's nemeton is golden like the setting sun over a field of barleycorn, shining with the wealth of love and abundance she draws in to nourish and validate her soul. Within a moment, the heavy swathes of blue fall away from the waif completely, as she is taken, shivering, into her golden glow of protection.*

*It's a temporary measure. I watch the dependence with tenderness, though not so much towards the two now holding hands, as towards all humanity: we find ways of surviving.*

*My contemplation is suddenly broken by a hand upon my arm and I'm acutely aware of my own nemeton flinching as I turn to see who has reached for my attention.*

---

Trust is not something our culture does very well. Even that point of energy meeting, nemeton to nemeton, can be hard to do, revealing as it does a good deal of the truth about who we are in terms of our soul's nakedness. Yet only through perfect trust is one of the most exquisite elements of Druidry revealed: *awen*.

Awen is often defined as flowing spirit, and through the Welsh etymologically this is reasonably sound. Yet such a definition seems simplistic, far from expressing the exquisite power the word denotes. Spirit energy in flow is the essence of life; waking to it can be extraordinarily inspiring. For me, it is not enough.

Having learned to approach another soul with honour, accepting the edges of their nemeton with respectful awareness, then with clear consent coming together so that those edges may touch, the energy, tension, the vibration, the colour of their surface shimmering through us, we can take the next step. This is the nature of deep sacred relationship: in trust with another, we surrender to the perfect presence of the moment, consensually to open the circles of our intimate space to each other, both sacred sanctuaries opening, creating one.

Without the veils and barriers that hide us, what we reveal is unspoken honesty more complete and brilliant than is possible to share in any other way. Like lightning to the soul, we are hit with the force of spirit as it touches spirit. Our essence touches and is touched by the essence of another. The pure energy of life and truth floods through us, screaming, howling, singing like thunder through the widest skies.

This is awen: spirit connection in absolute truth.

There are times in life when we open up so fully utterly intuitively, as a reflex reaction to a magical connection. In serenity and silence, for example, enchanted by the beauty of the sun as it sets golden over the frosty new-sown fields of springtime, our gentle yet total focus disguises the fact that we are completely open, vulnerable, breathing in the exquisite vision with every cell of our body and soul. Any moment of deep meditation might be the same. It would be easy to feel intruded upon, suddenly unsafe, disturbed to the point of being shaken, and simply by some instance that would otherwise feel trivial.

We do it too when we are gripped by any intense and passionate power of human nature. When we fall for someone, love overwhelms our normal cautions, making us blind to danger or threat, inspiring us to believe that anything is possible and, indeed, acceptable. We fling open the doors of our nemeton, revealing our sacred sanctuary and our self, and if we are lucky the one we love opens in the same way, so that together we share an instinctive embrace that may last an hour or two, a few days, six months or a couple of years, times of glorious blind faith, until the passion drug fades; we begin to feel consciously vulnerable and, often tacitly, we close ourselves up again. Thus our close relationships begin with a flurry of intimacy and openness, eventually to settle into a comfortable distance, detached, easy with familiarity but no longer deeply inspiring.

If we are conscious of what we are doing, finding the trust and then opening up our sanctuary for another to share in the intimate truth of our soul's song, we can also be aware of just when we start to close those doors again. If it is appropriate to close them, we can make that choice actively; if it is unnecessary fear or habit that propels us to detach ourselves, we can equally arrest the process, sometimes allowing the intensity and passion of our intimate relationships to be sustained, reinspired.

If it is anger that overwhelms us, tearing our nemeton open with its claws of self-expression, awareness here too allows us to make choices as to how we release the energy without creating unwanted havoc and destruction. Fear and grief more often close us down, but sometimes detrimentally, disallowing help, action, progress, release. The nemeton is controlled by no one but ourselves.

The most exquisite awen comes from opening and sharing the nemeton in a way that is utterly consensual, when both parties are aware of their edges touching, their boundaries opening, and the purest energy of life flows freely. Yet, when we open and another enters into our intimate space while remaining closed, still protected, not trusting or wanting to disclose his own soul, there is the danger of hurt. The same is true if we stay closed when another opens in trust to us, revealing their truth when we are unwilling to reciprocate.

In relationships that are perpetual tugs of power, where one partner is controlling, the other emotionally submissive, the nemetons reveal the situation clearly. After trauma, in illness, in grief, a person is often in the hands of a therapist, medic or carer, her nemeton open, broken: the rate of recovery can be acutely dependent on how that is handled, and although intuitively the one holding may be aware of the vulnerability, working the nemeton consciously can make a distinct difference. At times of confusion, we can be wide open, and an experienced con artist will be aware of how to bleed the situation. Many people, after losing the intimate embrace of their mother's nemeton, spend their lives seeking such one-sided comfort again. Manipulation and abuse are so easy with this soul vulnerability.

Becoming conscious of our own nemeton, strengthening the

edges with the rich invulnerability of our spirit energy, we learn how to protect ourselves without paranoia or defensiveness. We learn how to open, to love and to trust, in ways that are relevant and appropriate. We take control, for in doing so we become responsible for our own reality of relationships, and for the nourishment and inspiration that flows through them.

Needless to say, the Druid's relationships are not only with other human beings. Finding trust, we open our sanctuary to the earth, the wind, the old willow by the river. As our spirit grows and all need for constructed boundaries dissolves, the threads that connect us to all nature open in trust, each and every one flowing with awen.

---

*The dog's mercury is softly pushing through the musky leaf mould, splashes of yellow celandines littering the mud, stiff green shoots of the bluebell leaves that will cover the ground, but the day is beginning earlier than I would wish. I miss the long nights of winter's embrace on these cold mornings. The air is still biting with frost but not yet warm nor lifted by the scent of growth. The songs of the land are sharp, without the harmonies of green abundance.*

*Writing in my journal with gloved hands, I am breathing mist over the page. I shift my bottom between the tree's roots, a shudder of cold moving through me, and wish I could put into words all I feel and hear.*

*After a while, with a sigh, putting my pen to the ground, I pick up my flute. I don't inhale before I play, instead allowing the natural rhythm of my breath to add to the music. Nor do I seek out notes or tunes I have played before. With my fingers on the pipe, I open my circle to listen. I sense the oak, in whose sanctuary I have been sitting, whose sap is just starting to rise, pausing, thinking, feeling the light on old grey bark, reaching for warmth in the mud of the land, roots beneath me; the oak's song touches the nerves of my spine, beginning to hum in my bones, my fingers, my breath, and slowly the music emerges from the flute, like incense rising from newly lit charcoal.*

*And where roots intertwine with roots below, branches above growing through bare branches, I find different tones of the song that flow down through my fingers, the music I play husky, breathy, soft as the early light.*

*The drift of notes continues through me in silence.*

*I'm about to open my eyes when I hear the pad of paws on the mud and cold twigs behind me. The certain steps give me a clue as to who it is, and my hunch is confirmed when he makes that noise badgers make, a sharp, frustrated sigh, as if he's decided to accept a situation he's not altogether pleased with.*

*When I open my eyes, he is not more than four yards away from me, an adult, well over two feet long, from nose to tail. He stares at me, suspicious. A collared dove rises onto squeaky wings and flaps away above us, but he takes no notice, his focus intently placed on me. Nervous of frightening him away, I realize I've closed my nemeton: I'm glinting with uncertainty. Without moving a muscle, I breathe out into the ground, relaxing slowly and gently opening my circle once again. Breathing trust, I hold my focus on the oak, the earth, the canopy above, every little part of the moment right here. The subtle perfection of how every twig and stone, every leaf, spider, shoot and scent connect together, so intricately, fills my mind.*

*He scratches a belly itch.*

*I put the flute to my lips again, opening my soul to hear the notes of this creature. But, as I do so, he comes closer. Another itch.*

*You are beautiful, I murmur.*

*He looks up, straight at me, and he growls, then snorts with contempt, and potters away, disappearing into the undergrowth.*

*I blew it: I commented.*

---

Generally we speak of the nemeton as having one edge, but of course, in common with so much in nature, it is like an onion with very many layers of different qualities and textures. While trauma can break us open to the core before we are able to cope with that level of nakedness, when we make the journey of our own discovery, we open those layers steadily, deliberately.

Whatever causes us to open, it is vulnerability we encounter. In time that vulnerability eases as we become accustomed to the sensation of being open and honest, and our spirit grows in strength, but it never goes away completely, for truth doesn't exist on just one level. With each new layer we are able to reach, we access a deeper truth of our own soul, and truth is tender in its nakedness when first revealed. As we walk the path, we find treasures in those depths that come to light gradually, and each new understanding is sheathed in a delicate skin. The quest has no end but one we choose for ourselves.

Yet even with that tenderness, where we are able to share energy with another on each deeper level, the power of the awen is that much greater. Each new encounter that floods us with awen, spirit touching spirit, blows our mind with inspiration, strengthening our core. As we study the Craft of sacred relationship, it reveals to us the trust and truth necessary to inspire our journey upon the path. Through the exquisite brilliance of spirit that evokes such awe, the energy of life better understood, the nourishment of such profound interaction, we quest broader and more consistent perspectives of connection and nature's sanctity.

A stone may be easily picked up and hurled away without much thought, but if we take a moment to acknowledge its spirit energy, if we make ourselves aware of the geologically slow pulsing chords of its soul song, it is harder to dismiss it with a flick of the hand. This is not to idealize or get sentimental anthropomorphizing pebbles: they are still small chunks of rock. Equally, we no longer stamp through the forest, pulling at branches, breaking off twigs without a thought, or laze on the lawn removing petals from daisies or pulling up grass by the roots as a fidget to accompany our inner thoughts. No longer is it comfortable to swat a wasp dead simply because its curiosity is irritating. The connection between the cleanly plastic-wrapped meat in the supermarket and the blood and consciousness of the animal becomes more apparent, less easy to dismiss.

Through our growing ability to be open, to touch fully, and to hear, we rediscover not only the richness of our senses and the sensations they allow us, but also a respect for life in everything around us. It is only then that we move to consider the next of our physical senses: sight. An important reason for waiting until now is simply that, because so very much of our brain is wired to process visual input, this sense is the one we are generally least awake to. If we are reasonably sighted, we are seeing all the time, often hopelessly inattentively. Even with our eyes closed or in the dark, the visual nerves are stimulated by our imagination, images continuing to flutter through our minds. In our study, we leave it until now specifically so that we can appreciate its true value.

It is easy to test the idea. If we hear something first, not superficially but soul-deep, allowing ourselves to be washed with the sound vibrations of its music, when we see it the experience is that much richer. Hearing a story, a song, the wind in the trees, the laughter of a tiny child, the hum of a bumble bee – or the scream of a woman's grief, the squeal of an animal's fear, the cleaving and tearing of bark as a tree is felled – when we open our eyes to see what is happening, the moment is far more powerful, the images reaching far more deeply into our soul. Seeing fully, in a sacred manner, adds extraordinarily to the value of our life experience.

As in the case of the other senses, we were not only kindling our torpid brain to the physical input, not just learning to see more clearly with our eyes. We come to see spirit. Yet this is not about being psychic! It is about being awake, no longer being numb with complacency and familiarity: like everything in Druidry, it is about presence and connection.

Feeling the shimmering of our own life energy, it is possible not just to see colours, shapes and movement, but also to see the *vibrancy* that is each of these. We can perceive the perpetual changes, form and colour emerging, ever responding to the threads of the web, adjusting, reacting, exchanging energy. The swollen leaf bud bursts, high up on the beech branch, the tender green breathing its first breath, touched by silver rain, the rose-gold of dawn's sunlight, the laughter of the wind. The butterfly dances on the warmth of the breeze, scarlet and bronze flickering, so filled with purpose, leaving skitty streaks of life in the air. Nothing is stagnant, either in its emergence nor its decay. Every soul is richly coloured with its history, breathing the colours of life, leaving colourful traces in time and space along the way.

Such words, heard superficially, may be dismissed as poetic. Yet they are words that express again the sense that the Druid does not revere either creator or creation, but the ongoing vitality of creating. This is its dynamism. To one who has felt the current of awen that floods through the soul, shimmering with iridescence, sourced in the ecstasy of both beauty or pain, the poetry is an acknowledged side effect.

Just as the bardic facet of Druidcraft is focused on the mysteries of listening and the magic of sound and words, so the ovatic guides us to learn how to see. The ovatic: this is the second stage of Druid training and another area of practice within the tradition.

The word *ovate* is not as often heard outside Druidry as the word *bard*. This has much to do with the nature of the ovate's work, which was more quickly and comprehensively overwhelmed by the commercial and patriarchal wheels of monotheistic religion and science, particularly medicine. The ovate of our ancestors' communities was essentially the seer. Her role was to perceive a situation more clearly than others could, and so to foretell or cut a path into the future. She was (and is still) the natural philosopher, questing understanding and intuition about the natural world in order to respond more acutely, effectively and respectfully.

According to the oldest texts, and in tune with most modern teaching practice of Druidry, the ovate has already spent some years studying to be a bard. She may have little natural skill in that area of the Craft, but it is still considered essential that she knows the mysteries of sound vibration, of hearing someone's stories, of the magic of her own words spoken aloud. She has learned how to hear before she learns how to see.

In the modern tradition, the ovate is the one who holds the sick, the mad, the dying. She is midwife to the mother giving birth, and she journeys a little way with those leaving life: she has blood on her hands. She meanders with those on the edge of their sanity, pointing out the road when we lose our way. A therapist, counsellor or one who reads signs, omens, cards, bones, sticks or tea leaves, or simply uses a little eleventh percentile perception, she utilizes what tools she has to clarify her vision. She may be carer and companion, and healer too, using her deep sight to see how a person's energy is flowing, where it is blocked and cracking, leaking or dissipating, and what can be done to aid it.

She may work with animals, with spirits of the dead, energies, powers of the land, with the tides and the moon, with the skies and weather, seeking patterns, currents and flows. She sees rain before it arrives, and where lightning has struck. She may have studied botany, and the healing qualities of herbs and trees: she has mud on her hands.

Her focus may not necessarily be healing. In her vision of spirit and the colours of the soul, the ovate may also be an artist, using any silent medium. Crafting in paint, wood, charcoal, clay, textile or stone, she reproduces the images of her ovatic vision, offering them to those who have inspired her creativity, inspiring others along the way. In colour, she explores the truth of her own soul's expression.

Whether she sees with her eyes, physically, the energies of a soul and spirit, or sees with her belly, her feet or fingers, feeling pressure in her soul, it makes no difference. In any given situation, in the souls of those around her she is likely to perceive tension and disease, gaping wounds, leaking energy, brittle defences, in the humans and other animals, in the trees, plants, water and land. Watching with the sensitivity of her vision, able to breathe in the energy, the colours, the pain, she learns the harrowing craft of empathy. With consent, she may touch, stepping into another's colours, hearing their song, seeing the world through the other's eyes. Then, equipped with an intuitive sense of their situation, she is sometimes able to join them on their journey, now and then clearing the path upon which they walk. Often it is not possible or appropriate to sustain that closeness, and instead she uses her vision to shift the currents of a soul's energy, adjusting the nemeton's quality, offering ease, trust and calm. At times her touch is the brutal and catalytic scythe of change, an expression of her understanding of death and regeneration.

It is not an easy path. In the vast majority of situations, along the course of everyday life, her work is not requested. She sees the pain but has no right to intervene. Change may be beyond her ability. Finding other ways in which to express the suffering she sees, as well as the wonder and glory of nature, is an important part of ovatic work. For though at first she may be driven by a need to save or heal the world, through the power of presence she also learns acceptance. She makes a difference by expressing and perhaps changing the energy elsewhere, through the colours of her art, dance, photography, ceramics, cookery; in sharing her wisdom, understanding and awe, she knows that every thought and action touches the web of spirit.

We can *always* make a difference.

⟞⬦⟝

*'I don't know if it's . . . depressing or not,' she murmurs slowly. Her voice is small and hoarse, her throat racked from coughing. 'I can see that big tree . . . on the edge of the lane . . . opening its leaves and I know it's . . . singing and summer is . . . coming, but . . .'*

*Standing by the window, I can see the thickening green of the undergrowth, hawthorn and hazel, blackthorn and elm, and beneath them I know the bluebells and white stitchwort are flowering, the first of the pink campions. But none of this rush of new life can she see from where she lies, none but the grey of the bare oak and ash canopy, and that one vast old horse chestnut, the first tall tree to come into leaf.*

*I close the curtains a little more, muting the light as she's asked, and turn to sit back on the side of the bed. 'New life,' I smile.*

*'Yes,' she sighs, 'and when I'm . . . not feeling . . . ' She keeps stopping to breathe, 'bloody sorry for myself . . . or*

*guilty or . . . it is a good thing.' She lifts a trembling hand to her chest. I watch as her thin fingers gently push into the holes in her nemeton, wide black crevasses quarried out by the cancer and now this infection. A shudder goes through her energy and then suddenly she's coughing, and in an instant her calm is gone, her reason drowned by the crashing wave of fear, as that animal instinct to survive grabs her by the throat, choking her with panic. My words would make no difference, that creature having no verbal language − it flails wildly for breath through the tension of its desperation − and instead I hold my nemeton around her own, gentle in my own truth, calming the fear. The fit lasts but a few minutes.*

*We breathe together for a while, she now using the oxygen. I take her hand, running my fingers up her arm to the place that calms her lungs, sitting quietly with her through the moment. I've encountered death myself enough times to know what it tastes like, to know the silence that it brings, muting the sounds of the living. Here inside the battered remnants of her circle, my eyes closed, breathing steadily as if for the two of us, I can see the emptiness ahead: empty of pain, empty of distraction, empty of noise and weight and the gnawing of uncertainty. Empty. I let my breath settle us into calm. She squeezes my hand. I open my eyes. A woman is standing at the base of the bed.*

*'Aaah?' she asks, through the crackling of her breathing:* Do you see her?

*I nod and smile. This must be the grandmother she's told me she's seen before. It must be strange to have had no second sight before, to be given it now so close to death. She seems to me a beautifully strong woman, steady with love. I untangle the hand that clutches mine, leaving my fingers gently on hers, and slowly but clearly take my nemeton from around her. For a moment, her breathing rises and she begins to stutter into the raw pain of coughing.*

*'No, honey,' I murmur. 'It's OK.'* She isn't here to take you. You've still time. *'Let her hold you.'*

*While she sleeps, I watch her. Now and then, almost without thinking, I reach out a hand and brush my fingers over her, a few inches from her body, as if soothing down the fur of a dishevelled little cat.*

*I can no longer see her dead grandmother in any kind of human form. Instead I see this dying woman wrapped in a shawl of rich indigo blue, the colour of a clear midnight sky after a long and vicious storm. Still breathing, but no longer shimmering with her life, I can almost see what is left of her soul presence as glinting stars in that midnight sky.*

<hr />

On the whole, if we are to accompany someone on their journey through pain, trauma, healing or extraordinary moments of breakthrough, realization and release, we need to have experienced similar paths ourselves. I have been counselled by consultants and given advice by therapists who have no personal experience whatsoever in terms of chronic and acute pain, high sensitivity or the eleventh percentile, and at times I have smiled gently and filed their ideas in the dustbin; at other times I've gazed at them, bewildered by the arrogance of their assumptions as they attempt to help.

In Druidry, the issue of diversity is again here celebrated. An ovate may be well versed in herbalism or nutrition, working with solid ingredients and problems that manifest overtly. He may feel most comfortable and effective working homeopathically, using minute doses of remedy that act as simple witnesses to enable a sacred relationship to evolve. The spirit touches spirit, a vibration altering vibration, essence blending with essence, allowing a subtle yet powerful change to occur so deep down that the ripples move slowly through every part of the soul, affecting the entire body. He may work with no witness at all, simply calling upon spirit to be present, working with energies that emerge from the imagination and inner connections, yet even with this subtlety he may have no intuition or wisdom about pain or dying, for he himself has never surfed those currents at all.

There is no central school that trains and certificates an ovate as competent. He may have studied with this college or that teacher, yet still be useless at the Craft. His reputation, his own life journey and his ability to turn his own experience and knowledge into practical wisdom are all he has to justify his work. As such, with integrity of truth, he can pretend to be nothing but what he is. So is one ovate a profound healer and source of inspiration in a situation, where another would be out of his depth or even frustrated by the superficial level of the problems. One ovate might work with death and pain most effectively, another focus on physical malady, another on regeneration and rebirth, another on chaos and insanity, and yet another on dance or paint or cookery.

We differentiate here, however, between experience and understanding. There is a wisdom within Druidry that is much used by the ovate, where a little empathy is possible without comprehension. It is based on truth, and also upon nature's wide accepting balance of darkness and light, day and night, death and life, and the easy way that nature moves from one into the other through its myriad shades of grey on the tides of black and white.

Truth, in Western culture, is understood only to be validated by knowledge. We shine the torch of consciousness upon a situation in order to establish certainty in facts. The truth comes to *light*, clearly revealed in all that it appears to be, so that we might grasp it with confidence.

Yet in Druidry, seldom is anything declared to be fact. As an oral tradition, value is found in the transience and the subjectivity of the tale, an event brought to life by the emotional input and word magic of the specific bard who tells his story in the context of the here and now. There is no pretence about objective truth.

Of course, truth well lit is important. Gathering information about a situation can be crucial and is, indeed, an integral part of the Druid's learning. Yet truth can also be found in darkness. Through the mystical ovatic skill of seeing without seeing, perceiving without light, truth can be found in what we don't know, and even in what can never be known. There may be no understanding, no reference points, no immediate confirmation through others' agreement; analysis may be futile. Yet still, in this darkness, we can find the surety of truth.

It's a personal truth. Universal truth requires light and shared understanding in order to establish the widest acceptance, but in Druidry there is no need for this. *Dark* truth is accepted because it is based on experience, and in particular experience that is profoundly and consciously connected to the web of spirit. Inspired by a momentary union or within a long-evolving connection, the energy flowing through every thread is acknowledged as relevant. When we intuitively know something to be true, if that feeling emerges from the integrity of a wide network of sacred relationships, within which we are fully listening, with empathy and responsibility, then we have found truth.

Studying the Craft, awen-blessed connections are initially not easy to achieve, but when we are clearly following our own unlit paths of idiosyncratic and intuitive truth it feels even harder. Yet nature does not work within Western culture's limited perception. The meadow of wild flowers scatters orange and scarlet amidst purple and yellow, all set against azure blue skies, but the colours don't clash. Within the web, in time and space, they shine. Nature teaches us of the power of truth and diversity. Society teaches us to compromise in order to fit in, to not sing out of tune.

The wildness of our soul is the part that will not be pacified. Unkempt, ragged, unadorned, barefoot or completely naked, she runs amok in her exuberant individuality, devoid of inhibition, carefree and reckless. She lives on truth, both dark and light. Only sedated will she cease to itch and twitch inside us and, to most of us, sedation is the easiest way. Yet here is our creativity in its most raw and pure form, and to find a way to release it into free expression is a key part of Druidic practice, for to do so honours all that has guided us to be who we are.

There is a more profound wildness, too: our *wilderness*. The word is sometimes used to describe a barren place, yet such connotations express the arrogance of humanity and its blinkered and self-centric view of fertility. The wilderness of our soul is the one place inside that remains unaffected and unchanged by others. It is as precious and sacred a place as nature allows. Our song of this inner wilderness is as close to our own soul truth as we can find.

As a child, unwounded, we express that wilderness openly, with the courage of naiveté, curious at the impact of others on its energy. However, as our nemeton closes and we find our own boundaries, we come to protect our wilderness with all the wit and strength of our soul. Some people feel they have failed to do this, having laid it open to be abused and consumed by the bulldozers of social need and others' expectations. Yet a little part always remains, even if in some it is so deeply hidden as to be almost beyond reach (almost . . .).

Where the wild, untamed and unchained soul plays, in her own unspoiled wilderness, there is exquisite beauty and complete freedom. If we can access it, to wander and explore, drinking deep its clean air, it is a temple within that offers truly profound nourishment and inspiration. If we can dance its energy into our outer world, we sprinkle the glinting stardust of life everywhere.

Yet still we crave connection. We cannot live in isolation. These deepest parts of our soul long to be touched and to touch, spirit to virgin spirit, to feel the flow of awen upon the web of life. The wild soul aches for connections that are wholly ecstatic, sacred relationship, awen blessed, in the uninhibited exploration of life. She wants to dance in the rain, to stamp in deep puddles, to love without fear, spinning with music and colour and realization, dissolving into sensuality, dark truth and understanding . . . and not always alone. Releasing her creative expression from the depths of her intimate space, the most sacred temple of her nemeton, there are moments when the wild soul wants to share.

If we can overcome the fear, opening the barriers of our sanctuary to another soul, lifting the veils to the extent of revealing our wildness and our inner wilderness can be glorious. To do so with a conscious congruence, integrating the physical, emotional and mental, as well as the spiritual layers of our being, only goes to intensify the experience of connection. It can fill us with a bubbling surf of energy that craves release in laughter – crazy, free, belly-shaking laughter! – yet which can also be directed into any medium of creativity. Or it can fill us with a deeper energy, one that can move through our physicality as an amazingly erotic sensuality, the awen touching us in a way that stimulates the erogenous intimacy of our soul.

Making this divinely inspired connection with another human being often breaks apart the conventions of social acceptability. The awen is so strong that gender is irrelevant, for the poignance of touch is primarily spirit to spirit, energy rising like a storm at sea calling for release through physical expression. The norms, lies and hypocrisies of heterosexuality, monogamy and unimaginative sexual coupling are joyfully discarded, together with their sticky threads of shame and guilt. Instead, unhindered by such artificial limitations, the awen flows, encouraging us to explore the furthest reaches of human sensuality.

This freedom is easily held within the fabric of Druid morality: the vision of the web of complete connectivity and the responsibility that is intrinsic to that web, together with the inherent respect for life in all its diverse forms, and the sanctity and nemeton sanctuary of each individual soul upon its own path of life. Yet, through the understanding of this respect for individuality, honesty is considered paramount, and more pertinent than generic and social rules or convention.

Druidry simply does not judge the expression of creativity of any soul, in its art or physicality, its gender or sexuality, nor does it measure one soul's creativity against another's, for it seeks no artificial construct of perfection or normality. Celebrating diversity, it teaches us to honour life.

I end this chapter with what, for some, may be a challenging idea. Yet again it is at the heart of the Druid tradition.

Sensuality is not restricted to connections between human beings, either in nature or in the Craft of Druidry. Though sexuality, as physically intimate interaction, is something we hold within human relationships, profound and erotic sensuality need not be so limited.

Geoerotic or ecoerotic experience, the art of opening the soul to the pure spirit energy of plants and trees, of earth, sea and sky, can be both exquisitely pleasurable and profoundly transformational.

Indeed, for one who is yet to learn how to trust another human being, it can be a good deal easier and more satisfying to be soul naked with a young ash tree as it dances in the wind, or a bent old yew, blood-red from the rain, or a wide, sun-warmed rock beneath open skies, the softness of wet mud, the moonlight that seems to open the soul with a silver blade, or the thunder, with rain pouring, streaming, pounding . . .

———⟫•⟪———

*. . . my face upturned, eyes closed in the force of it, each great, cool drop shattering into a thousand droplets on my skin, over my lips, water sliding over my teeth, sweet, soft water – I laugh as I drink it in, tantalized, enthralled by the sensation with every nerve awake to the touch, drops gliding so slowly down my neck, finding their way into my dress, already drenched down to the hem and suddenly so stiff and enclosing . . . the stretch of pulling it up and over my head is a glorious freedom, and I drop it to the muddy ground, tingling in my body nakedness, the rain now shattering against all I am, and I laugh aloud at my socks and boots, sniffing the water from my face, untying laces, pulling them off as the storm streams over my back, then feeling the cool mud under my feet, my toes . . . and with the sensations heightened, I'm so aware of the scents, the musky earth, the wet bark, the stems of elderflowers heavy with rain . . . and again I stretch, my hair clinging to my face and shoulders, as I reach out and open again with my breath, unzipping my body, my hips swaying with the rhythm of my blood, my hands adding to the rain's caress, soft and cool on the curves of my body, slipping into its warmth, as I dance to the wild, thundering music of the storm . . .*

# Chapter Five

# Powers of Nature: Gods of sun, tree and dewdrop

Druid deity is a profoundly different concept from the monotheist creed. Although we use the pagan Germanic word (from *Gott*) or the pagan Latin (from *deus*), the word has been commandeered by monotheistic religions to mean God: superhuman being, supreme power, ruler of the universe. Druid deity does not have a capital *g*.

The semitic idea of *oneness*, one rule maker, one God, has so thoroughly infiltrated our culture that it is difficult for some to perceive it, let alone discard it completely. Even secular society encourages us to seek out and conform to the oneness: one leader, one truth, one way of life, one answer to the ultimate question. It is as if the human mind, breaking into its self-awareness, desperately struggles in its need for order; we want to tidy away the dirty chaos of nature, putting it into a catalogue of boxes, neat and contained, controlled, controllable, graspable and refutable. To the outsider it seems monotheisms carefully place the capital *g* God into this same box-tidy system and, labelled INFALLIBLE, keep it out of reach of humanity; yet those who do this appear to be so scared of nature that they themselves crave supreme power to control it. In most cultures where this God is deposed, the act is done by humans who, through wit and brutality, claim for themselves such power anyway.

In modern Hinduism, there are now theologians who speak of the tradition's adherents revering one god by many names. The same is true in some areas of Druidry and other modern Paganisms. In the search for order, there is a sense that polytheism, like animism, is a backward way of looking at the world; evolution surely guides us to the civilized and clear-cut view of the monotheist. It is an attitude that is widespread. Endorsing profound prejudice, both overt and subconscious, sometimes bitterly shocking, it would be offensive if it didn't so clearly reveal such a complete lack of understanding. Acknowledgement of the crucially different paradigm has not been made.

For many, Druidry is unambiguously polytheistic: it accepts that there are not one but countless gods. As far as archaeologists and historians can access and understand the clues left by time, Druidry always has been polytheistic, and it continues to be so. Yet, just as I am no longer required to perform animal sacrifice, as a Druid priest would have been a thousand years ago, my contemporary of that era would not have counselled communities and guided acolytes by email three thousand miles across the world: the tradition has evolved. The vision of deity has evolved, too, yet not with monotheism as an endpoint.

This process of its evolution is about our changing attitude towards control and authority. The fundamental definition of deity is unchanged: a Druid god is not an energy that controls nature, it *is* a power of nature.

In millennia past, a Druid may well have cowered, submitting and subservient to wild and rampaging force of nature, to a cataclysmic storm, a killing plague, a burning drought. There are areas of the world where little has changed, where nature is still a constant threat, where death sits snarling on your shoulder, where life is brutal and utterly mysterious; in such harsh realities, the priest responds within his own context. He reaches out to the forces of nature in a language that he himself understands, imagining gods in human form yet with power beyond any man; gods with whom bargains might be made, whose discontent might be appeased, who might be placated by shows of humility, submission and subservience.

Yet in Western culture, our world has changed, following the course of our evolution. With the twenty-first century opening before us, our lives are held by a measure of certainty: comfort and dignity are better assured than they have ever been. Science has offered us a catalogue of feasible explanations, most of which add to the comfort extended by predictability, physical healing and shelter from the rage of the elements. We are released from constant fear.

Priests in the Druidic tradition no longer submit.

A Druid doesn't worship her gods, head bowed and obedient. She doesn't charge or ascribe them with authority over her or over her humanity. The animistic tenet that teaches an equality of attitude towards all things is mirrored here once again through the understanding that there is no hierarchy in the world: only individuality, unique perceptions, strengths and weaknesses, skills to share. A cat or beetle, snake, badger, tree or person, a cloud or wave, all have equal rights to respect, and so do the gods. Each entity, each spirit, each force of life and being, is acknowledged as wholly distinct, celebrated in its singularity, in its perfect uniquity. Even when we are faced with something that obviously has more overt power than we do, it is acknowledged as *difference*, not superiority.

Indeed, the very concept of a supreme or supernatural authority seems to most Druids both ludicrous and unnecessary. The animist acknowledges all things – trees, stones, winds, stars, human beings, butterflies – as essentially comprised of spirit, life energy that flows through time and space upon a soul journey of intention, at times leaving traces in matter, the creativity of physical form. There is no doubt in his mind that this life energy is sacred, yet it is sacred in itself: he holds no desire to find a supranatural and all-knowing consciousness beyond nature that guides, judges or controls it. Within a spirituality that reveres nature, the very idea that such a God could or would exist is surreal: wholly implausible. Only with that understanding in place can we begin to grasp the quality of Pagan deity.

That isn't to say that in Druidry there is not deep respect and reverence for power, and even sublime surrender into relationship with deity. To define deity in Pagan Druidry, we need to distinguish what is god from what is simply the sanctity of spirit that hums throughout all nature. This defining process is an important one, for it is crucial to the process of finding our morality and how we choose to live. One key is simply this: gods kill.

———◦◦◦———

*With eyes closed, entranced by the smooth, cool rock beneath me, the sounds of the water rushing, swirling by, I feel the tug again in my soul. Reluctantly I open my eyes to a day that feels too bright, despite the layers of thick, pale cloud that cover up the sky. That tug again: my bobcat, one of the felines of my soul, is pulling for my attention. My eyes settle on the forest across the river, the rich colours of maples, beech and pine, birch leaves flittering in the slightest breeze.*

*But . . . she pulls at me. She loves these New England forests, her body and soul alive with the scents of other bobcats to seek out and avoid. I sigh, feeling sated with the ease of the moment, letting my consciousness wander downriver to where the water is serene, glassily reflecting the shadows of the sky. Then slowly, placidly, I turn to make my way back against the current, up towards where my body sits upon its cool hard rock. Passing it by, down close to the water, I feel the energy and excitement and, intoxicated in the mist of ions, the cold touch of fine splashing surf, I slip into the white foam where the currents are finding their own ways around and over the rocks and stones, tumbling and dancing, diving, eager for it all. The flow is strong against me, trying to pull me with it, and for a while I resist, pushing against the flood, hovering where I* am, just above the surface. Then I let go, my resistance breaks and suddenly the river is pouring through me: like a jug being filled eternally with the first flush of cool fresh beer, I am overwhelmed with its sating energy, its wild exuberance of spirit. It rushes through me, clearing, cleansing, sluicing my body, washing straight through: I'm breathless with it, emptied out but for the cool sparkling and wonder.

Then I breathe out. It's been a while since I breathed at all, and as I do so I dissolve, slipping silently through its wild energy, down under the fast currents, into the black force of the river water. Its weight rises around me, dark as night and fully holding. Every sense of my body is subsumed by its being. A part of me senses that I could move according to my own will, but for a moment I am enthralled in the completeness of this embrace. Letting go of a little more control I am taken into the extraordinary intensity of this deep current; the reality of its power is like a force of gross coercion and, tumbling over myself, I'm suddenly crashing, battered and ribboned by the rocks hidden deep in the dark. I can't breathe. I'm gulping water unable even to swallow, kicking limbs in every direction yet barely moving at all. I can't tell which way is up, all I want to do is scream, but the weight is getting heavier and all I seem to be is sinking . . .

Then, suddenly I'm exploding through the surface, shattering the silent pressure, gasping for breath, crying out . . . daddy! . . . And again she tugs me. I open my eyes, and the deep amber brown of my bobcat's stare meets me, a paw poised above the water. She taps it once again, not liking the wet but poignantly calling, little drips falling from her outstretched claws.

I hear you, I whisper.

And sighing, I slide back into my human body, this chilled form of flesh and blood that is sitting still on the hard, damp stone at the water's edge. Memories: a number of times as a child I had almost drowned, and for a moment I sit there with the memories falling through me, settling like late spring snowflakes in my soul.

I look out over the black water, innocently sliding by.

*I had danced with the eddies and swirls, currents and splashes:*
*sprites flittering, laughing, playing, prying, finding their way in*
*the collective gathering of water, between air and stone, utterly*
*within the luxurious and momentary cohesion of it all. Yet I had*
*slid through that energy into the integrity of the river's own*
*power. Not spinning and exploring, its intention was all river.*
*I breathe in.*

I hear you . . .

*And what before in me was wonder now shifts, slipping down*
*onto more solid ground, rooted deep in my ancestry, my*
*certainty, my soul. The ecstasy of my play was glorious, healing,*
*freeing. But now it is irrelevant: a child dancing, skipping,*
*yelling in the silent gravitas of a temple at dusk.*

*I sit, my soul within my body, feeling the breeze on my skin*
*and the hard stone against my bones, and I breathe, here, with the*
*river.*

*Together.*

---

For millennia, rivers have been seen as deity. The Saco River
(mentioned above) showed me her power. In my own land, I have
been taught wisdom and beauty by the River Thames – that most
sacred waterway which, flowing from west to east, cuts clear across
the south of Britain; but I have also known people who have died
in it and the many streams, brooks and rivers that pour their flow
into it. Perhaps because I am ever mindful of its power, it is more
distinctly a part of my focus as a priest.

Beyond rivers, the Druid polytheist reveres as deity the sun,
oceans and seas, fire, lightning, frost and cold. These are easy to
understand according to the definition of a deity as a force that can
kill. Those who live or have lived in earthquake zones or near
active volcanoes, as I have, know that the earth too can kill. They
are powers of nature whose *ishness*, whose soul intention, is not
affected by humanity and cannot be tamed by humanity, and
whose action can at times take lives, one by one or in swathes.

Scientifically, we can pick out elements, chemical reactions, reaching down to the atomic level and beyond, and point out that each of the above is a culmination of more basic forces. Yet the Druid, each priest and seeker, finds his own relationships, his own experiential and ecstatic bonds with the gods around him. Each individual, through her own distinct perceptions, works with what she is capable of waking to and connecting with, soul meeting soul, spirit touching spirit.

A mountain as a divine entity is a gathering of elemental forces, each adding to the energy that gives it its holistic power. We might engage deeply with the mud, the rocks over which we clamber, the crystal that glints in the sunlight as we climb, the wind that chills, the metallic purity of the streams that slake our thirst, the prickling, gale-blessed shrubs that scratch and draw blood, the broad energy of the landscape breathing all around, the thinning air, the snow and ice. To the Druid, the mountain is deity, because it gathers within its soul song all this power of life and death.

If I pose the idea of a virus being a deity, too, I sense some people would recoil. A drop of water may not kill, but an ocean of drops can easily do so, and especially so if the ocean's song starts to weave with that of the wind and all that moves the tides into their extremes. Is it that a virus en masse could surely never be glorious as an ocean can be? Yet, to one who studies its power of regeneration and colonization, a virus can be intensely beautiful: perhaps terrifying, but beautiful. Or is that flinch of aversion because a god surely should be something one can love? Yet this is not a Druid notion. Powers of nature are simply that: tremendous forces that move through our environment, raw, dark, giving, warming, holding, brutal, annihilating.

Of course, not all that kills is deity. The number 53 from Hackney is not a god: it's a public omnibus, albeit with the potential to wear you out or run you down. This is not dogma; I am not laying down rules that must be followed, only presenting a key that suggests how we might distinguish deity from other spirits.

So what of those forces that are said to be gods who don't appear to be that powerful or to have killing inbuilt? The power of birthing can be seen as a deity; ever conscious of the shadow, the Druid honours this power because it so readily kills both mother and infant. The Green Man, god of growth and vegetation, the summer exuberance of verdancy, keenly smothers and strangles, as one plant finds nutrients, space and light to the detriment of another. Nor is his power restricted to competition within the plant realms, for his roots break up concrete, his heedless breathing suffocates rivers, his strength erases pathways and crops, his soul celebrates in spikes, prickles and poisons. The soil is a god too, with the rain and the sun, for the flow of their combined songs will feed us, and at times they will not: the culmination here is honoured as gods of fertility and nourishment.

To me, the forest is deity, here where I live, and this brings us to another aspect of that key to what is a god. A force of nature whose energy flows perpetually through this sacred valley, with hazel, sweet chestnut, oak and ash, and with its springs of clear water adding to the deep fertility of the soil, the forest was a crucial part of the livelihood of the community here for thousands of years. Yet now few people ever enter it, and those who walk their dogs there keep to the wide human paths that mark its perimeter. Nor in itself is it dangerous; if on a moonless winter night, black darkness about me, I were to lose way back to the track, it would be exposure to the cold rather than the forest that killed me. Nonetheless, it is deity to me.

This is because without the forest, not only would countless thousands of creatures die, but the soul of this valley would die also, and a part of me with it. It is poetically said that as Druids, as priests of the land and the ancestors, it is our obligation to tell the stories of the old gods. Some take this as a necessity to retell the myths of our heritage, those of Bran, Bloddeuwedd, Arthur, Morgan le Fey, which is indeed important, and about which I shall speak in the next chapter. However, the obligation has a deeper meaning.

The stories are not only those of old mythology; they are also those of the land. And without their tales being told, it is not only that the old gods die, but we do too. Deity, then, is that which we *must* respect in order to survive. We can't afford not to. It is not only that which we cannot chain or tame, whose nemeton is greater than us, whose power is beyond us: we honour as deity that which we must not abuse, with our greed of consumption and fear of chaos, or we shall die with it.

So are the forests understood to be gods – and the rivers and moorlands, the tundra and desert, deep caverns of gems and fossils, the seas, the planet's atmosphere, the very earth herself. Life is sacred, and each ecosystem is dependent on a delicate balance of life. To mess with that balance is to dishonour the deity the place embodies. Without respect, humanity pollutes, destroys, irrevocably altering the harmonies and rhythms of nature, jeopardizing the sustainability of all life, wreaking havoc for the sake of a short-term alleviation of fear.

With an intellectual, thoughtful attitude, we can all do our best to be environmentally conscientious; yet when this secular social responsibility is deepened into spiritual recognition of the divine, there is no need for careful thinking. Our behaviour is intuitive, guided by our profound connection, rich with devotion, love and honour. Nor can this be an artificial construct, for that too would be contradictory to Druid philosophy: though at first we might hold ideas, it is not belief (or guilt) that motivates, but the experience of relationship with deity on which our environmental responsibility is established. That which we love and respect, soul to soul, we cherish.

Relationship is everything.

While I have met a few priests and wise folk who have deep relationships with what they perceive as God, a single divine force, what I sense in most are still specific facets of nature: most commonly a local earth or vegetation deity. However, another reason why polytheists don't reach for this oneness is that one force would be too big to be anything to human consciousness but an abstract concept, and we cannot forge an ecstatic relationship with an abstract.

Some reply to my challenge by explaining their vision of deity as a wholeness rather than a oneness, often using the term *pantheism*. Sensitively describing a theological vision that holds an understanding of one deity, in pantheism God is in everything and everything is an aspect of God. A good many mystics of diverse religious traditions have subscribed to this view in one way or other. It would be an acceptable vision within my own Paganism, but that in order to understand it fully I must use that capital *g*, deity becoming universal. In this vision of pantheism, God is still the one supreme force, the one power that creates, holds and destroys.

There is a further pantheistic notion held by some, that God does not exist outside of or separate from nature. Potentially this removes the idea of a capital *g* God, while not denying the concept of deity altogether. Deity is the sentient energy of life, the conscious force that flows through all existence. However, for me this is still too close to a monotheistic and therefore limiting vision. While I can understand how the energy of life could be generalized into a oneness, within Druid theology this energy has no purpose, no intent, no direction, nor consciousness. It shimmers within the universe, yet doesn't guide or control.

This is the crucial point: life energy, expressed as spirit or deity, is the smallest building block, not the largest.

Making relationships with wind, rain, sunshine, moon or mud, the many layers of our being can be moved, touched and changed, from skin to spirit, from the emotional to the ethereal. By reaching for the incredible power of a particular force of nature – something we can feel physically, internally or externally – and through surrendering by opening our nemeton protection so that we can experience it soul-deep, the wildness in us can be truly nourished. For there is no illusion, no need for belief, no opportunity for doubt: what we feel upon our skin is the warmth of the sun, what we feel within is the stirring of energy, and that is enough to inspire our reverence, as we reach out for connection.

'Hail, so do I call to you, powers of the east, breath of life, you who sing through our every sound, wind that dances through the tall trees, you who teach of freedom's flight, let us feel your presence within this rite, I ask you. . . ' In the dawn's silence around me I whisper, keenly aware of my own voice. I breathe in and close my eyes, my hands raised towards the hills over which the sun will shortly rise, my soul open to all that I have ever learned, the mnemonics of my words filling the reach of my invocation. The air I breathe is sweet; it clears my throat and energizes me, enticing me to stretch my shoulder blades, poignantly aware of my wide, black raven wings opening out, taut with heavy anticipation to catch the wind. And I wait, a few seconds perhaps, but it could have been minutes, for it didn't matter. When the flurry of a breeze rises, shimmering through the wet grass, I smile, whispering, 'Welcome,' and I turn to face the couple.

Beautiful in their love, in leafy crowns of elderflowers, roses and lilies, their young faces alive with the cool air and the emotion, they look into me, open in their shared intimacy. And as I pose the challenge of the east, '… through times of uncertainty, winds of change …' they squeeze each other's hands, answering with tenderness, with sincerity, with all the world before them and no knowledge of what they will face, 'I will,' I will love and honour you, even when I have no idea, no sense of direction, no certainty, powers of the east … And I nod that I have witnessed this vow made, and add my voice to the breeze, 'Then may you be blessed by the powers of the east, the clear air of dawn, the freedom of high skies … laughter, new light, clarity, inspiration, renewal … may your marriage be blessed by each new dawn.'

Without a noise, he crouches to the ground and, moving his hands over the wet grass, his eyes closed, he murmurs a prayer. Then standing, he touches her face, his fingertips wet with the cool dew, and her eyes sparkle. Moving the hem of her long robe, she does the same, reaching up to his face and leaving trails of water that glow on his soul. And together they whisper to each other, *breathless in the intimacy of their shared nemeton, 'Blessings of dawn.'*

*Though at each of the cardinal directions, having invoked the powers of nature, they had made vows and shared the blessings, it is the east that she speaks of later when we are warming ourselves by the hearth, sipping tea. He sits at her feet on the floor, holding one of her feet with one hand, his mug with the other. The steam rises in soft sunshine.*

*Her eyes are still shining, awake with wonder, 'It was as if the whole of dawn, every single thing that dawn has ever been, it all touched me in that moment. The sun hadn't even risen, at least not so as we could see it, but . . . it was like the air that went into my lungs.'*

*'Into every pore . . .' he adds, softly, putting his hand onto his belly. 'It felt like I was breathing through every part of my body.'*

*She smiles at him, 'Yeah, the air was so pure and alive and new . . .'*

*'It was like, in that moment, our vows, our wedding rite, was touched by the goddess,' he says.*

*'You were,' I nod, 'you were touched by the goddess of dawn.'*

---

In Chapter 6 I shall explore the gods of *human* nature, of anger, love, beauty, hunger, but here let us again affirm that there is no anthropomorphization, no projection of human qualities upon the powers of nature outside humanity. The *ishness* of the sun, its nature and flow of existence, has nothing to do with human consciousness or some supernatural force, and everything to do with isotopes of hydrogen fusing into atoms of helium, kicking off neutrons and massive amounts of energy.

Where a deity is named, stories told implying he has human form and language, it is allegorical, the poetry of prayer and the lyricism needed upon the road to understanding. Where we can't use our highly developed powers of visual processing to grasp something that seems abstract or mysterious, we create pictures, forms and images in order to increase our comprehension. Equally, where a deity of nature is gendered, this is also poetic. In reaching for a deeper connection, qualities of one gender or another (as we perceive them) are glimpsed, brought out or superimposed. As a language, poetry is magical in its ability to lay down bridges between the spatial and rational sides of our brain, the limbic and neocortical, the emotional and analytical: it uses music and imagery to clarify and soften the sharp edges of words.

Nor are there human ethics involved or imagined in our perception of Druid gods. Our relationship with the gods of nature is one that is inspired and not directive; an ocean cares nothing for humanity beyond the subtleties of energy connections along the web. Sitting with it, feeling its energy, hearing the songs of its journey, we can find the awen that inspires and guides us with our problems — and where we can achieve a deep and sacred relationship, a magically open connection, soul to soul, that inspiration is intensified. The ocean is a divine spirit whose energy is focused through the creativity of moving water; it won't give us clear solutions to our very human questions.

These are important issues; for, if we get stuck in the sticky details of others' visions and experience, we can quickly find ourselves trying to accept or believe in something that doesn't settle naturally within us. Acknowledging that the language is poetic and not a way of expressing fact, we can listen with honour and perhaps find inspiration in what we hear, inspiration that adds to our own understanding, courage and progress in terms of connection and relationship.

The alternative is dogma, which is anathema to Druidry. It is dogma that takes us into the complicated and negative connotations of *religion*.

I used to take 'religion' to be the questing for deity, but if that is the case then those traditions without clear concepts of deity, such as Buddhism, fail to qualify. The definition of religion as being a spiritual and ethical language that binds people together makes sense to me; Druidry clearly brings people together. This is not through a need for external or social affirmation with regard to beliefs, for it holds no beliefs lacking rational or scientific backing that might need the support of a faith and community to maintain. There are no gods, no God, no metaphysical or supernatural idea that each seeker within the tradition must subscribe to. As a result, Druidry can often appear to the outsider from another path more like an attitude or philosophy than a religion.

Yet Druidry does inspire that religious bond of community. Affirming the journey of the individual, acknowledging each personal experience and vision, the bond is the sharing of a spiritual literacy and terminology of the quest, and an ethical perspective that is so often in contradiction to the mainstream culture of consumerism and competition. Based on the Druid's profound respect and love of nature, the bond is celebrated in the Druidic language of ritual and creativity used to express nature as sacred.

Looking at the gods of nature, we come to a profoundly significant and poignant issue that separates Druidry from other spiritual traditions, including other Paganisms: Druidry contains no theology of a beginning or end of existence. There is no original creator whose being fragmented into the myriad spirits that became creation, or whose craving to see a reflection of him/herself generated the universe. Any myths found in the library of modern Druid writings or storytelling have been put together in the last few hundred years, and most in the last thirty years. And I object to them all.

For I see this as one of the most exciting aspects of the tradition. Existence simply is. If there was an initial force, a beginning, the Craft holds no need to find or understand it: so far from scientific or empirical spirituality, it is irrelevant. The deep mystery that we must engage in is that we are here; our focus is not how or why we got here, but what we do now that we *are* here. Our purpose is not to reach heaven or get off the wheel of lifetimes, but to learn how to live *now* in truth, freedom and ecstasy.

The linear mentality of creation to apocalypse, birth to death, generates within it an attitude of competition, bullying and hustling, as if life were a race to be won – and the winning were crucial. Instead of the kick-off, the fight and the final scoring up, in Druidry there is just the game, endlessly played. Our soul journey continues, expressing itself in its many forms of creativity (as human, as cat or tree, as spirit in the wind), always fully connected with the web through genes, time and basic energy. Indeed, my great love of the art of medieval Celtic knotwork is due to its expression of that perfect sense of eternity. Such an understanding of existence provokes an entirely different way of being: release comes through *acceptance*. Responsibility, presence and cooperation, sustainability and connection, mutual benefit and nourishment become the essential keys to living.

Instead of linearity, we talk of cycles. Indeed, letting the words most often used in the tradition here flow into a pool ... cycles, circles, spirals, seasons, tides, the ebb and flow ... we can easily see how intimately the philosophy of Druidry is connected with the island landscape in which it is so deeply rooted.

In Britain, the temperate climate is so stubbornly temperamental that we frequently have at least four or five seasons competing with each other, sliding in rapidly one after the other, swirling around the same moment in time; sunshine, thick mist, warm breezes and snow can all find their way into the course of one short day. Such a climate creates an ecology where nothing is ever the same. Each time I look at my garden, leaves are blowing in a different direction, flowers have turned following the sun, colours have altered their hues according to the light and moisture, temperature and wind. Change is everywhere, and all the time.

Lying between latitudes 50° and 61° north (New York is at 41°; Vancouver, Canada, at 50°; Melbourne, Australia, 38°S), dusk in Britain can take an hour from fading light to night falling, with dawn equally long. At midsummer, where I live in the heart of the island, although the sun sets at around 9.45 p.m., dusk taking us to summer's twilight at around 10.45 p.m., it is never dark, and the light of dawn is easily seen on the north-east horizon by 3 a.m. In the middle of December, the day arrives not much before 9 a.m.

and is already fading by 3.15 p.m. More pronounced than the tides of temperature or humidity, and usually utterly out of synch with them, these tides of light and dark ebbing and flowing through the year add to the magic of the tradition rooted within them.

Inspired by this dynamism of nature's cycles, Druidry is truly a spirituality of change. The human instinct for survival is understood to be powerful, but in many ways the instinct for familiarity is even stronger: too often an individual will remain in a terribly destructive situation because it feels safer there (with the 'devil we know') than to make the changes needed to get away and move on. Our ability to imagine the future allows us an equal capacity for fear. Change can be terrifying, provoking the apathy, catatonia and defensive aggression that is so much a part of our culture.

The teachings of the Druid tradition, however, actively guide us through change. Giving support through the initial point of release, holding us in the crisis of emptiness as the past is torn away and nothing is understood, then leading us into the time of regeneration, reconnection, integration and growth once more, the Craft journeys with us through the cycles and seasons of our lives.

Yet these aren't tools of personal development and psychotherapeutic analysis, or empowerment exercises that work on the mental level, focusing wholly on self. The magic of Druidcraft comes through our developing relationships with the natural world around us, and crucially through our ability to maintain those relationships through the crises of life. In openly trusting and intimate connection, walking in rhythm with the cycles of nature, we find an internal stability amidst the flow and chaos of change. In ritual, pausing from the rush of living to step back and remember the sacred, the Druid learns to dance in rhythm with the natural world around her. As she gets to know better the subtle lores of nature, so does that reflect upon her understanding of herself. Celebrating the cycles and tides of the gods that move around her, she gains congruence through those reflections, dismantling the barriers that separate the environment she lives in from that which flows within her own body and soul.

Druidry encourages us to make that ritual pause in order to honour the changing moments as they pass through the course of each day – acknowledging the rising of the sun, its height at noon, through to sunset and the dark of night – finding our natural points of energy and of stillness.

Aware of the lunar cycles, the Druid may make ritual at any time, from its fat fullness to its time of darkness or the first sliver of the crescent. A ritual may be formally performed, predesigned or completely wild: the importance is not in the theatre of the ritual as much as in the ongoing consciousness of the cycles themselves. With both male and female hormones surging and receding with the lunar tides, controlling the flows of menstruation, emotion, sociability and energy, an awareness of the moon allows us not to suppress or fight the tides within ourselves, but instead to move in tune with them.

Awareness of barometric pressure and air humidity can be equally disruptive to a wild and sensitive soul: spending time with a group of children on a day near the full moon when the air pressure is rising fast will reveal to anyone the powerful effect it can have! To have a consciousness of this natural force is deeply empowering. We don't need to be able to change it, but we can learn how to rise with it, to open out and stretch, or to quieten, not resisting the need to turn inwards, understanding the energies that are playing upon us.

Looking at the cycle of the year, modern Druidry advocates the honouring of four seasonal and four solar festivals. This is the cycle of eight specific days that was devised by Ross Nichols in the 1940s and brought into Druidry in the sixties. Although there is valid historical and archaeological evidence for each being celebrated in millennia past, there would have been no concept of a community acknowledging the eight days. It is the ease and wealth of our Western culture that enables us to pour our energy into a major festival every five to seven weeks throughout the year; yet, poignantly, it is also the increased distance from nature with which we live our lives that makes it so much a necessary part of the tradition now.

The year begins at Alban Arthan, the festival of darkness and the rebirth of the sun. Usually celebrated from the eve of the winter solstice (astronomically falling around 20 to 22 December) and for the following few days until midwinter's day (23 to 25 December), this is a rite rich with community spirit, involving the sharing of resources, gifts and feasting. We honour the winter darkness and cold that holds us close to home, limiting the reach of our lives, offering an emptiness and the opportunity for renewal and fresh beginnings.

Imbolc, or Gwyl Fair, is the first festival of spring, a seasonal rite celebrated calendrically on 2 February, but often at the closest new or full moon. Some celebrate with the sighting of the first wild snowdrops in bloom, or other native spring flowers: that which signals the power of natural regeneration through the depths of the cold. Imbolc is a celebration of new life, of our dreams for the growing cycle ahead, the inspiration that holds us firm even at this coldest time of the year.

The solar rite of the spring equinox, Alban Eilir, falls between 20 and 23 March, a time in Britain when the landscape is blessed with yellow flowers, as if each bloom were calling to the growing strength of the sun. It is a time when we begin to look out of ourselves again, more naturally reaching beyond the confines of our home community, starting to seed new ideas.

Beltane, Bealteine, or Calan Mai, comes calendrically on 31 April to 1 May, though many people celebrate with the nearest full moon or the flowering of the hawthorn (which, where I live, can come anytime in the three weeks between mid-April and early May). Beltane is a time of exuberance, with life emerging now without inhibition, the energy of fertility spreading through the land; it is a festival of sexuality, of self-expression and the freedom of soul creativity.

Alban Hefin is the solar festival celebrated over the three days of the summer solstice (falling between 20 and 23 June) to midsummer's day. A time of power and self-assertion, it honours the height of the summer sun and the warmth and growth yet to come.

Lammas, Lughnasadh, or Gwyl Awst, is the festival that draws our attention to the harvest, guiding us to look at all we've poured into the growing season, all we've nurtured and are now starting to reap. After the loud, lazy time of midsummer, Lammas is a time of hard work, celebrated on 1 August, though often honoured at the full moon or at the first cutting of the principal local or staple crop.

Alban Elfed is the autumn equinox which occurs at some point between 20 and 23 September and, with the main harvest in, it is a time when we've a sense of whether it has been a successful year or not.

Samhain, Samhuinn, or Calan Gaeaf, is the closing of the year. Celebrated on 31 October to 2 November, at the nearest dark or full moon, or with the coming of the first frost, this is the festival of the chaos of leaf fall, when temperatures have dropped sufficiently to bring the ice claws of frost that kill back the last of the year's growth. It is a time of release, of closure, of honouring the dead.

Between Samhain and Alban Arthan is the time of the dead. Rich with stillness, with darkness, emptiness, the potential that lies within, it is a time without distractions, a time to cut back to the bones of honesty once more. With its Christmas lights and the gaudy noise of glossy, voracious and unnecessary consumerism, how our culture hides from the power of this time!

Including long, cold winter nights, snowy mornings and spiders' webs, tough green shoots breaking through the frost, coy snowdrops and wide, grey days, spring's exuberant pale tenderness and flower-budding growth, summer's lethargy and warm, scented nights, the golden moonlight of harvest, sweet, sticky fruit, cool mushrooms and leaf fall – these dates and images are relevant for Britain.

Across the northern hemisphere seasons vary with local winds, tides and flora guiding the dates of the festivals, and in landscapes of the southern hemisphere and the tropics, the differences can be even more distinct. Thus some Druidic groups find it effective to turn the traditional calendar of eight days 180 degrees, so celebrating Beltane at the beginning of November, and so on. Yet in climates where the summer is a time of dearth, the vegetation burnt out by the heat of the sun, it is the autumn, not spring when the songs of new life are sung, calling to the powers of regeneration and abundance. In tune with the teachings of Druidry, it is in our forging of relationships with the environment that we learn when and how and where to honour and celebrate the turning cycle of the year; once again, dogma is not only irrelevant but irreverent.

Others prefer to reach into the magic of the tradition's history and, wherever they live on this globe, they celebrate in time with the seasons of Britain. Here we find a form of the tradition with a focus more firmly placed upon the ancestors than the landscape, and this must also be acknowledged as a path for those seeking wisdom in honour.

---

*The sunlight flickers through the beech leaves, still translucent with soft, new growth, touching the forest floor almost with a tenderness, as if reaching out caresses, yet anxious to see if they're accepted. I stretch, wanting to breathe in more fully this first sensuous gold warmth of the year, but so careful not to crush a single one of the countless bluebells that surround us, this wash of purple-blue quivering in the dappled sunshine.*

*He sighs beside me, his eyes closed. His nemeton is tinged with the bluebell's blue and he lies open to the beauty. I lean back to lie beside him, draping limbs across him in our relaxed embrace, sinking into his energy with love and trust.*

*For a long while we are quiet and still; a deer wanders close, the fawn by her side acutely alert, taking in every scent and noise. I can feel its energy, its new life so awake to the world. Their measured footsteps pause and move on, crackling twigs on the dry mud yet not disturbing the calm of the forest. Bird song, souls singing their territory and pride, lifts the air, souls as invisible as their nests, camouflaged in the spreading canopy and shaggy undergrowth.*

*With the lazy curiosity of my deep contentment, I watch the*

*bluebells. Each one seems to drink in the sun's touch with a
focused intensity, not letting a drop of light escape should it dance
its way, each draught drawn down deep into the thick leaves that
cover the leaf mould of the forest floor. Yet the apparent
nonchalance of the bluebells makes me smile. Only the occasional
young bulb's flower, deep blue upon a thin young stem, appears to
reach eagerly for the light, its fey song shimmering above the hum
of the rest, unashamed of its pleasure and its thirst for more.*

*And I turn to my lover, conscious now of a part of me
desperate for attention, for the pleasure of his gaze, his touch.
Like a young bluebell, I crave more than I need, suddenly
wondering how much my soul can take, eager to drink in an
ocean of love. We've been lying on this boat, paddling our fingers
in the water; now I want to capsize it, to dive deep in the quest
for uninhibited passion and surrender.*

*'What are you up to?' he murmurs, feeling me twitchy with
energy.*

*'Summer's coming . . .'*

*'Skitty cat . . .'*

*I shimmy my body closer, moving over him, so I'm looking
down into his face. 'It's exciting,' I smile.*

*'Welcome summer,' he whispers, and pulls me towards him.*

---

In our hectic lives, we are constantly stumbling over moments
when we would do better to pause, to stop and think, then stop
thinking, breathing deeply of life before stepping back into its
currents again. We can do that every six weeks in the fullness of
festival rites shared with others, but only by finding that stillness
regularly will it become a part of our lives. So does Druidry
encourage us to pause a good number of times every day, until
making those connections becomes a part of our natural vision, the
neural pathways in our brains secured, the positive nourishment
affirmed. Indeed, if we understand the basis of Pagan Druid ritual
to be the simple craft of describing the moment and the place in

which we stand, honouring the spirits and powers of nature, the essence of life, and so finding its sanctity, there is no need for formal ceremony: just focus and a little time.

When the cycles of nature are not so obvious, for instance in the cityscapes of our world, this is even more important. Without radical changes in light, the full force of storm and wind, the easily seen path of the sun and moon, the practice of Druidry is not only far harder but even more essential. After all, the gods are often no less present; they are simply harder to perceive amidst the chaos and distraction of human and urban sprawl.

It takes wakefulness to see the trees clearly, as spirit brilliance, as souls moving upon their own path of intention, investing their creativity in the grey and brick of the city. The weeds that push their roots into soil-filled chinks and gaps, the birds using our buildings as cliffs, the bats in our attics, the foxes and rodents: all are thriving upon the flows of nature in the city. The gods of vegetation are there, deities of skies and rain, the earth goddess still *thrumming* despite layers of brick and concrete.

Creating and tending an altar to the spirits of place and the gods of nature is a key part of daily practice for any urban Druid. Ensuring that it is constantly fresh cultivates our wakefulness, helping us to keep awake, listening and watching, finding inspiration in the most unexpected places. Not only do we make an immediate acknowledgement of what we have discovered – a crow feather, a current of wind, the course of an old river now flowing underground, the colours of the sky upon a glass building – but taking something of it to our altar encourages us to further that relationship, deepening our connection to the powers that have moved through that place for perhaps thousands of years.

In such environments, it is easy to allow our focus to slip entirely towards the gods of human nature. Yet when we do so, our lives and our attitudes become profoundly out of balance. We cannot live in isolation. Holding our connections and our reverence for the gods of nature beyond humanity, even those that are no apparent immediate threat to us, is the only way our species has a hope of surviving.

# Chapter Six

# Powers Within: Gods of love, war and plastic

If we understand the gods of Druidry to be powers of nature, and accept that within the tradition there is ever the quest to find balance and congruence between our internal self and our external environment, then our focus cannot only be upon nature beyond humanity. A religious tradition that, by definition, reveres nature, reveres too those sacred forces that constitute *human* nature.

Once again, I speak of *reverence*. This is not worship or submission. It is an attitude that is thoroughly infused with respect, open to awe and the clear thrill of wonder, willing to feel and to show love, and receptive to learning. Without the self-dismissal of submission, this reverence is ever wakeful to how that power flows through us as individuals, affecting the experience of our journey, directing the course of our life.

*A sharp tingling of pain shoots through the sensory glands at the back of my jaws, my mouth suddenly wet with anticipation, and almost breathless I'm looking up at the droplet of juice that builds. Even as she laughs, like bubbles, there is a serene stillness around us, a sanctity of this moment of sensuality and sharing, and her head moves back, soft curls of hair falling over her shoulders, as the sun that was behind her breaks over my face. Blinded and washed over by its warmth, my eyes closed, my mouth open, I smile as that long, rich-red drop breaks over my lips and teeth. It's sweet and sharp and so bright with spirit that I feel my body waking, my soul unfolding.*

*Then mischief takes over. Feeling the sun's glare gone, I open my eyes in the shadow of her face in time to see her squeezing another strawberry, this time crushing its flesh into mush right over my face. 'Oi . . .' I start to object, but she's giggling, jumping to her feet, and gone before I can grab her. Rolling onto my side in the white flowering clover, I watch as barefoot she runs, her little legs carrying her off into spinning games of summer laughter.*

*I can remember so clearly the last time I ran, three years ago, before the pain took away the option. I remember the exhilaration of having broken through the pain-fear to let my body take me chasing the football across the field. My son had stopped and watched me, then run to where I'd collapsed in a heap, to hug me, amazed and tender with affection. 'Be careful,' he'd whispered, ten years old.*

*I pick up a strawberry between finger and thumb and gaze at it for a while: the pocks and seeds, the brilliance of its colour, and I gaze at the lines, crinkles and scars on my skin, the round, pink and white smoothness of my thumbnail, and I move my fingers, watching them, their silence and motion, now so often numb, the skin browned by the sun . . .*

*Then, closing my eyes, lying back in the sunshine, I bite into the fruit.*

The body is extraordinary. Impossibly complex, beautifully crafted, by treating our own with care and reverence we honour both our ancestors and all who inspire the ongoing creativity that it expresses.

Yet it is the forces that flow within us that drive us along our path, and in Druidry it is these that we refer to as the gods of human nature. These are the gods of lust, of love and sensuality, of anger, hunger, fear and war, of death and violence, of mischief, laughter and play, of birthing, holding, grief and sanctuary, of trade and poetry, of healing and courage, glory, truth, divination and deceit. The list goes on.

Not all of them, of course, are the exclusive domain of humanity, but we are not seeking forces around which we can draw sharp lines. Firstly, because of the essential connectivity of all nature, each flow of nature seeps into others, currents blending, merging and transforming. Yet also, it is the way these natural forces play through the human psyche that allows them, at least in part, to be found upon this particular – albeit artificial – roll of gods.

We call these forces gods for just the same reason as we distinguish what are gods in the natural world beyond humanity: these are forces that can kill, that do kill, or which – without adequate respect – can and do kick back at us with intensity and destruction.

They are not human constructs. Like the gods of sun and thunder, they are not 'people'. They are forces of nature, powers that can brutalize and leave us shocked, shaking and desperate. They are not entities driven by a consciousness in any human sense of the word; they are energies in motion, distinctive in vibration, colour and tone, utterly enmeshed in the web of connectedness that is all life.

They are not figments of our imagination. Their power is very real and the Druid attitude to their sanctity ensures that these powers are acknowledged with adequate respect. They are powers that we reach into for the sweet relief of understanding, not least when we have experienced their wild energies coursing through our hearts and minds, taking our feet from under us, leaving their trails of devastation behind them. Like all gods of nature, we may find them upon a quest for knowledge and clarity, or in the darkness of intuitive truth and spirit-to-spirit connection. Either way, we learn the quality of the spirit energy that hums deep within, the specific pitch of that power, building a surety of familiarity and recognition of its presence. We come too to understand the nature of its intention, its journey and drive, for with no real cognition here we are all too easily swept up upon its currents, to be battered and used and abandoned along the way.

Just as with the ocean, or indeed any other power of nature, we can for a while allow a god of human nature to overwhelm us, choosing to slide in surrender through the holding, moving weight of its body, breathing in its soul song, in order to experience and learn, to find the awen ecstasy of deeper connection – but to submit would be to offer our lives, to offer to die, and times when such action is appropriate are few and far between. We can surrender into the power of love, anger or lust, submerging into its energy, letting it seep into every pore, but to lose ourselves in it *completely* would be to invite devastation.

Here too we find within Paganism the anthropomorphization of gods. I'll speak later of the gods of myth and legend, those clearly fashioned into human form, but I first encourage students of the tradition to find their own vision of the gods, before using others'. So often, those who seek out the gods, glimpsing or forging relationships, translate the divine energies they perceive and sculpt them into human figures, embellishing them with words and pictures, and adding glory in superhuman ability. By doing so they are following an ancient tradition: it does seem much easier to interact with a divine human entity than an abstract energy. With less fear and more recognition, however, understanding can be facilitated, allowing a more significant level of connection.

Indeed, as we are talking about gods of human nature, one might ask what the problem would be to draw such a divine force into human form. The gods are not human, however; they are energies that flow through humanity. As a metaphor, although what we perceive most clearly are the sounds of the rustling, shimmering leaves, it is the wind that is the force that moves them, a power invisible without the trees: the gods of human nature are like the wind, moving through the forests of humanity.

Giving gods human form is poetic; it can be beautiful and inspiring, but what we are seeing are merely the visions and creativity of an individual or those of an agreeing collective. Expressed through different soul songs and contexts, moments in time and space, such visions may well not attune or touch our own at all; indeed, to use them may well distract or limit our own ability to find that much sought-after connection. To me, such humanized ideas or pictures of the gods are always profoundly deficient, giving only a glimmer of insight into the power behind them. They can be useful, but only if that limitation is kept in mind.

Anthropomorphizing these gods can permit another delusion as well: that the gods of human nature care. At an inter-faith seminar I recently attended, having spoken enthusiastically of my own polytheism, I was later approached by a desperately nervous young man who stammeringly whispered the good news that 'there is one god who loves me'. Smiling curiously, I was about to ask which one, when I realized that what he had actually said was, 'there is one God who loves me'.

Urgently doing his evangelical duty, albeit in a profoundly inappropriate environment, the lad could not bear what I'd said, that the gods don't care. Indeed, following publication of my first book, *Spirits of the Sacred Grove* (republished for the US market as *Druid Priestess*), I was chastized by a group of feminist Witches from the West Coast of America for stating that there is no all-loving goddess. For those who hold such beliefs, my words would clearly be considered blasphemous or deluded, and a hand is reached out to me in anxiety and tender pity.

Yet that lack of care is an integral part of the potency of my Pagan Druid theology. Like the acceptance that there is no beginning and no end, the knowing that there is no loving *über*force in nature that will secure justice for us all provokes a clearer focus on the here and now, leaving us in possession of a germane and poignant personal responsibility. We cannot assume that nature will balance up the *good* with the *bad*, ensuring that everything will *be all right in the end*, for there are no such concepts outside the human psyche. Furthermore, the forces of human nature contain no more care or justice than do wind or plate tectonics.

Our human craving for safety immediately splashes questions upon these pages. For surely, if we are to acknowledge any divine being at all, there must exist a deity of love, whether he reveals himself in the form of the wise and gentle son of a Jewish carpenter, or she does so in the tenderness and lushly curvaceous thighs of a mother goddess.

Here I struggle a little with the limitations of the English language, and first would like to separate the idea of love from that of caring. After all, loving or being in love is far from a perpetual state of bliss. Love is brutal and beautiful. Its deepest soul purpose is that of breaking the barriers of our individuality, cracking open our nemeton sanctuary, in order to allow the wild ecstasy of merging utterly with another. Overwhelming us with emotional energy, it can drag us over hot coals of passion, only to drench us in cold water, leaving us soaked in sweat and lust and tears. It can tear us from the strength of our centre, pulling us so off balance that we exist leaning on the other, who in turn may precariously be leaning on us, and the slightest shudder of life beyond brings us collapsing to the rocky ground. Love is a powerful god. It doesn't care.

I would separate, too, the idea of family, the loyal son, the doting mother. For neither is the position of parent nor that of child invariably replete with caring. Filled with hopes and fears, and the integral and at times incessant struggle of reshuffling boundaries, not to mention the excruciating pain of birthing, the exhaustion of sleepless nights, the crises of separation and the deep uncertain angst of growing, for both parent and child family bonds may be blessed with caring, but it is not fundamental to their nature.

Of course, caring can be found in human nature; through love, empathy and even obligation, most human beings can access that current. It is not, however, a supreme force. It is simply one of the countless powers that make up the dark and chaotic energies of the natural world.

With the destructive and dangerous powers so openly acknowledged, and without the comfort of anthropomorphization or a belief in some principle of justice or loving goodness, Druidry celebrates life. One might question the sanity of reverence, let alone the idea of making connections with the wild and divine forces of human nature. What of violence, lust and rage?

As is the case for the gods beyond humanity – the gods of sun and rain and river – the Craft of Druidry teaches us not to submit or fight to tame or control these energies, but rather to reach for understanding sufficient to allow us relationship. We are guided to be able to recognize the energies and, with respect, to work with them, accepting the effects of that interaction without losing our own footfalls, without quashing our own soul song melody.

---

*Such things often happen within a strangely elastic length of time. As I turn, having felt my nemeton disturbed, a split second stretches out before me, allowing me to take in every last fine detail: his coat, lifted by the speed and spin of his fall, rises in a curve, following him round and down as he crashes heavily onto the ground. His face looks so calm, almost touched with curiosity, as if he himself is aware of how slowly he is moving, wondering how and why and where he might land. Then he closes his eyes, just before impact, the tiniest fraction of a second before his elbow smashes down, then his shoulder and hip, and I'm aware of my own body flinching in that instant's empathy.*

*Then noise fractures the stillness, shattering the image into smithereens that slide in every direction, too slowly but now screaming, and I turn to the car, slipping as it does through time, exhaust fumes, yellow street lights glinting on the rear window. And the anger inside me grows as slowly and as surely; I can feel the power of it as if, creeping quietly into my body, it unfurls down every limb, reaching into my fingertips, an energy that wears me as if I were its sleekly fitting suit of flesh and bones and circumstance. I can feel its heart thumping in my own, and*

*through my mind I know that something must be done. Suddenly*
*the anger breathes, and as it does the world races back into real*
*time, while I hurl over the car a net woven of rage,* STOP!

*It skids to a halt, and everything is dirty, fast and confusing,*
*as the driver jumps out, running back towards us, shouting, 'Are*
*you all right, shit, I didn't see him . . . ' And the anger breathes*
*me as I slide to the pavement beside the man I love. He's*
*mumbling raw expletives into the dust.*

*'Is he OK?'*

*I look up into the young stranger's face, 'You were driving*
*away.'*

*He's shaking, nervous, 'I . . . I didn't know what to do.'*

⟸⬥⟹

Facing the wild chaos of energies within human nature, we might
argue for logic, for the reason and sensibility of the human mind.
Yet from a Druid perspective these are aspects of our psyche not
loaded with nature's energy. They are not forces that *drive* us upon
a momentum: they are guides that *direct* us. A difficult idea to grasp,
it is nonetheless an important one. For while the gods are the
powerful energies whose purpose and intention move beneath us
and through us, we do have free will.

Remembering that I speak as a priest, and without the intention
of putting myself forward as a scientist, it is interesting to
contemplate the way our brains are constructed, for these powers
of human nature affect us in different ways and are thus
acknowledged differently within the tradition.

Simplistically dividing the brain into three, the oldest part is low
down at the back of the head. This base brain is reactive; like a
lizard, its behaviour is hard-wired into survival, finding sunshine to
warm the body, shelter to hide in and instinctively moving in the
quest for food. Though ever alert to attack or defend, with sharp
sensory input, it is not able to anticipate, yet not entirely erratic; it
succeeds by relying on simple habit.

The part of the brain that has developed from that is called the limbic brain. This is where the soul physiologically lays down its memories of experience, and consequently where we find the filing cabinets of our beliefs. The limbic brain perceives more broadly, its developed sense of the past peppering the present with anticipation, with expectation. It lays out concepts of ownership, reacting from its broader perspective with emotion. Communicating through music and dance, through art and ritual, the limbic brain is one of symbols, sounds and meaningful movements.

In humanity, bones from a hundred thousand years ago show that quite suddenly the brain doubled in size, and the so-called neocortex developed. From our still limited understanding, it seems that our species took another eighty thousand years or more before this new area of the brain was accessible with consciousness. The great leaps in terms of human evolution over the past dozen millennia are integral to this developing conscious use of our neocortex.

Instead of being reactive, a word derived from the Latin *agere* (to do), the neocortex is responsive, the Latin *spondere* (to vow or promise) implying a consciousness and dedication. No longer always walking into the unknown, suddenly opening before us we had the facility to envision the future. The neural pathways of this high front end of the brain gave us the ability to conceptualize, to abstract and rationalize. Verbal and mathematical language unfolded, with science and logic following on, and advancing beyond all previous constraints.

Hand in hand with these things came that definitively human characteristic: consciousness of self. Perceiving the future, we imagine our own journey through it, beginning with a vision of our current state. Yet the self-centricity of that vision doesn't automatically comprehend or hold in awareness just how we are linked to everything around us. With self-consciousness comes an awareness of being alone, a sense of separation. Indeed, some say that it was this neocortical evolutionary step, and the self-defending human arrogance it quickly engendered, that provoked the rift that still lies between humanity and nature. Certainly, the neocortex allows us to judge and to make decisions based on those judgements, and that sense of separation does provoke a limbic emotional reaction that feeds back into the neocortex, informing its next decision. Both make mistakes, but both are wholly interconnected.

The limbic brain behaves according to a hierarchy of stored beliefs. The wild bear breaks open the beehive because its positive experience of the honey is stronger than its negative experience of being stung, but this is not premeditated decision making. It's still very much about instant gratification. There is no neocortical intervention that allows the bear to judge possible outcomes, to weigh up options in order to decide. The neocortex, however, is a box of tools, fine precision instruments with which we are able to assess risk and value. Where the limbic brain leaps, the neocortex pauses to consider. Where beliefs provoke an emotional response that is propelling us towards action, the neocortex clarifies the situation, justifying or negating the emotional reaction, and formulating an appropriate response. Its reason guides us.

Although these distinctions are neither rigourous nor necessary, the gods of nature, of sun and rock, hunger and decay, are those of the base brain. There is no sense of separation from the environment within that primitive mind, and in part this connection, without boundaries, is what we seek in Druidcraft: not a return to a primeval pre-mammalian state, but the ability to access that oneness – yet to do so with a consciousness that is fully interwoven with the emotional and intellectual reaches of our brain. The rich depths of understanding and experience that we gain through such a connection are extraordinary, taking us into the dark, non-verbal mysteries of the Druid tradition. As the connection grows more familiar, the sacred soul-to-soul relationships developing, our consciousness finds increasing comfort and ease in this state, relaxing into the boundless nature of its congruence, its mental stillness and grounded freedom.

In turn, the gods of human nature can be seen as those of the limbic brain. To repeat the list given previously, they are lust, love, sensuality, anger, hunger, fear, war, death, violence, mischief, laughter, play, birthing, holding, grief, sanctuary, trade, poetry, healing, courage, glory, truth, divination, deceit ... Amidst a handful of human processes, this is a collection of human cravings and emotional reactions, beliefs provoking the fuel of arousal. From a Druidic theological perspective, these are divine forces.

I take a few to clarify my point, beginning with lust. An easy power to illustrate the nature of these gods, lust is a force of craving, a current that sweeps under us to propel us towards a source of relief. We may constrain it with reason or justify it with excuses, but its soul intention is the sacred flow of sexual hunger.

Deceit is a part of the powerful craving to hide, an emotional energy born of fear that inspires camouflage and retreat. Although we use our neocortex to devise all manner of complicated intrigues and lies, the force is limbic, a god of deception.

Mischief is another Druid deity, a natural flow that objects to predictability: an old favourite of mine, I like to think it is this energy that enables humanity to be so innovative and adaptive. Unwilling to accept boredom, inherently needing stimulus, it upsets apple carts and lets felines run free, with no special need for neocortical evaluation.

Divination? Another interesting power: using limbic imagery and ritual to ease the craving that is the quest for release from uncertainty and fear, this is a flow of nature that, as deity, is often termed a god of time. It is to this force that we might call in order to see through the linearity of chronological life and glimpse the future. To some, however, the powers accessed through divination are not of time, but of spirit vision, and here we find any number of gods who may be the motivating force, inspiring the ovatic seer to forge the necessary connections and relationships.

Trade is a little more complex, for it has been adapted and developed by the neocortex, yet in the old traditions there is still acknowledged a natural force, a god or gods of trade. We do need the ability to hold a concept of the future in order to anticipate gratification in some kinds of modern exchange, such as using credit cards on the Internet for something that will be delivered in twenty-eight days! Yet it is the immediate quenching of desire that is at the heart of all trade: *I get this* (if I give you that) *now*. A deity of trade embodies the energy that is this flow of exchange, and honouring the god can ease the process.

Money is a curious beast, too. In Druidry it is clearly acknowledged as a current of energy and one that allows that instant quenching so necessary in exchange. As a force of nature and a part of human culture for millennia, we might use the term currency (from the word *current*), for it need not be in sterling, dollars or euros: such objects as shells, stones, feathers and nuts have also been manifestations of this energy flow. In quality, I feel it is similar to an emotion such as anger. Usually considered negative, anger tends to be used aggressively, selfishly, and without adequate thought for the web of connectedness. Spat out by some in order to alleviate an immediate crisis, an expression of personal might and glory, it is held onto by others too scared to face it, hauled away deep inside, where it becomes harder to express. Yet, working with a god of anger, channelling the energy with poignance and rational intention, and most importantly with acute consciousness of the web of life, anger can be used as a powerful force, inciting change that is felt to be both positive and progressive.

Even similar in its vibration, money is used in a comparable way. An energy that allows action, motivating us through lack or abundance, calling in changes with its current, money can be used to fan out our defensive frills or courting feathers, or it can be stored away as a finite and precious energy, allowing us to feel plumper, padded, protected. Where it holds us, sustaining us, there is usually little change in the flow and little excess to provoke either trouble or change.

To the polytheistic mind, watching the consumerism of secular society, the cycles of greed and fear so evident, to say that money is not a god is a risible perspective. As with all gods, however, the modern Druid does not submit to its unceasing flood, worshipping with an obsequious hope that she will be chosen and rewarded. Just as we do with winter's ice, the forest's wood or the fertility of the land, we find a connection in order that we might live with it creatively, retaining our own balance, in harmony.

The word sanctuary was also on that list and here, at last, is where that deep desire for caring is met. With a natural current that embraces, sanctuary is a deity that holds us in sweet surety, and crucially so without a need for understanding.

---

*She clings to my hand. I raise the other, in a gesture that I usually do with both, speaking the words of the rite to all who are gathered in the circle, 'Let us here honour the spirits of this place, for they have accepted our presence and hold us in this moment with respect. Let us be awake to those who stands with us and around us . . .'*

*And as I talk, I look up into the dark murmuring of beech leaves, silhouetted against the night sky, moonless yet pale indigo with summer's underlying light. Stars blink through the flickering leaves, moving on a cool breeze – like a wildcat, it has emerged to hunt on silent paws after the heat of the day. As I breathe it in an owl calls through the trees, and she squeezes my hand tighter, crushing my fingers.*

*In their own time, those around the circle speak softly, honouring the clear, glinting light of the stars, the hawthorn beside us, '. . . the foxes of this wood . . .'*

*'. . . the holly whose fallen leaves keep pricking my bare feet, reminding me to listen . . .'*

*'. . . the sweet moisture in the earth, after such a hot day . . .'*

*'. . . the darkness that holds us . . .'*

*Their words interweave with each other, a soft play of sound, prayers and imagery, memories and gratitude, as some slip forwards, quiet in the night's stillness, to place offerings on the stone we've set as an altar: a crow's feather grass-threaded with a twig of fallen leaves, a plait of barley tied in with a few wild oats, a fat green apple (she bites it open at the altar, juice slipping down her chin), '. . . the wild raspberries . . .'*

*'. . . the nettles . . .'*

*'. . . the beetles scritching in the dry mud . . .'*

*Each word is given into sound with such poignant respect. And I hold the circle, my soul focus entirely coloured by the divine energy I feel. The name I use for her I would not speak aloud, but others call this power Nemetona, goddess of sanctuary, of the sacred grove, and from my belly her energy extends and embraces the temple circle, a place of serenity, stillness, beauty and peace, into which have gathered these few dozen women, each come to find their own here and now . . . including the one beside me, her eyes tightly shut in fear, her hand quietly crushing my own.*

*It is not unexpected. She is here in dark moon ritual to face that fear, provoked by a life scarred with abuse, and she has brought with her this force of fear, invoking it with her shuddering, holding onto it with her other hand. Momentarily, it reminds me of a rite I did with an evangelical Christian minister, a strange occasion where we were both asked to make blessings upon an assembly, giving thanks for all that had brought that (inter-faith) meeting together; there was an instant where I was aware of our gods facing each other across the grass, like two winds meeting, towering above us, swirling into what felt for a dreadful moment like the eye of a cyclone. In my sanctuary here, reaching over the sphere of serenity scribed and held by the beech canopy, the darkness, my soul and my goddess, this power of terror looms heavily, as if waiting.*

*I turn to her and smile, offering strength with acceptance, and see how the force of this fear is tied around her womb. 'Let's make offerings,' I whisper. She shakes her head, her feet clamped to the edge of the circle, I can't. 'Come on,' I say more firmly, You can. 'Watch the beauty of the altar. Now.' With her fingers almost breaking mine, she shuffles after me, and as I'd hoped, immediately she's away from the edge, the knot of fear slackens. She's inside the sanctuary fully, and I don't hesitate in sealing the temple bounds more securely. As we crouch at the altar, I smile again, offering her the crown of bramble we had made that afternoon, a brutally blood-hungry and beautiful circle of pink-tinged blossoms and chaotic thorns.*

*Slowly letting her fingers uncurl, she takes it from me,*

*undaunted by the prickles, and places it gently on the stone in the silence, the whole circle watching, holding the sanctity of the moment, affirming as they witness these precious moments. The glimmer of fear is clearly still alive in her womb, but it is no longer reaching out for the universal force, that great god of terror. I stretch my crushed fingers. A tear falls from her eye as she almost smiles.*

---

The nature of evil is not in my list of gods above. In many monotheistic theologies, and throughout dualistic culture, there is indeed acknowledged a force of evil, elevated by some to supernatural or superhero (super-*anti*hero) status. From that camp, Paganism itself has been considered an embodiment of this force, for it is perceived as distinctly detached from the authority of their one God or concept of goodness. In tune with the dualistic paranoia of 'if you aren't with us, you must be against us', the Pagan is indicted with being in league with the Devil (with a capital *d*). It's a charge that many of those who follow the old traditions still find offensive, but thankfully the heart of Druidry and other Paganisms now tends to shrug with a smile, for the idea is too ludicrous to warrant attention.

Evil is not a power of nature. The wind does not tear down a house or uproot a proud ancient oak through any sense of malice, yet nor is its action a mistake. Its intention is no more than to be wind, energy in motion. The power of love does not find its victim after careful consideration, embedding that deeply wounding arrow having decided whose life to shake apart with passion, yearning and bliss. Love is its own force, a wild river flowing through the landscape of human nature. The otter does not eat the trout alive because it enjoys the agonized squirming of the warm, fishy-sweet flesh: it is simply otter being natural otter, belly touched by hunger. Wind and love, hunger and otter, none are tapping into some evil force of the natural world that enables them to be destructive.

Since it is not a power of nature, evil is not a god of the Druid. It is not a part of the limbic brain where we find the urges and cravings of nature. When someone commits an act that we consider barbaric enough to be called *evil*, we most often judge it as such because of the person's premeditated intent: they have thought about what they were going to do, realized it would be damaging to others and continued regardless. Evil can be better defined as a deep flaw in the human psyche; for – now able to imagine the future, and aware of the ricochets of cause and effect – the neocortex has allowed us the ability to consider the consequences of our actions. Where the individual construes values and priorities that are too different from his contextual society, the society that will be affected by his actions, and he continues to live in accordance with his own values, that society can judge him or his behaviour to be evil.

When horrific occurrences happen and it is decided that there is not sufficient proof of consciousness to be certain the person knew the consequences of his actions, we are likely to lift the label of evil. He is then judged to have made mistakes based on ignorance, or to be too unwell to function in society. From the perspective of the seer of spirits, it can sometimes be the case that individuals are, often unknowingly, influenced by the dead, or by some toxic energy seeping from the earth, from stagnant water or memories of trauma still shimmering in the air. Here again are other reasons that provoke human beings into brutal behaviour, shifting brain chemicals, denying a man reason or the ability to enforce it.

When a head of state declares war knowing that thousands of innocent citizens will die, is his action justified, mistaken or evil? Is he sick with delusion? We can ask the same question of the suicide bomber who feels so profoundly about his beliefs, his own values and priorities, that he is willing to die to help the cause. We can ask it about the paedophile, the Amazon logger, the thieving drug addict, the supporter of fox hunting, the gay man in a state where homosexuality is illegal, or indeed the practising Pagan. All have been declared evil and will be again. Our answers will all reflect our own values.

Our answers reflect, too, our understanding of connection and the web of spirit. The word *sin* in Christianity clearly translates as separation or disconnection from God; in a tradition like Druidry where deity is nature, to be disconnected from the natural world and the web of life is to find oneself at risk of committing grievous mistakes, behaving in a way that may be seen as evil or 'sinful'. The subtitle of this chapter is a dig at this very issue, for although we can acknowledge love and aggression as powers of nature, plastic is a creation of humankind that seems in distinct contradiction to respectful and sustainable life. Products that will take millennia to decay naturally, that cause pollution in their making and their destruction, and are often wholly unnecessary, are in themselves an expression of humanity. Plastic, like evil, is simply another dreadful by-product of the fearful human soul.

In considering acts more likely to be globally considered evil, that flaw in the human mind is clearly affirmed. I don't raise examples, for it would be interesting for each reader to seek their own, finding those that aren't born of personal or cultural values. Whatever the act, to behave with this degree of gross barbarity requires an individual to be completely disconnected from the web of spirit. In such situations, it is detached curiosity, a quest to alleviate fear or isolation, forces that *are* limbic powers of human nature that drive such a broken individual: not evil.

I have not yet spoken of the gods whose names are held with pride across the Druid and other Pagan communities of the world: the British Rhiannon, Arianrhod, Cerridwen, Don, Bran and Llugh, the Irish Dagda, Dana and Morrigan, the Gaulish Taranis, Teutates and Esus, the Viking Odin, Freya, Loki and Thor, the Greek Hekate, Pan, Aphrodite and Demeter, and the Roman Venus, Diana and Mercury. The list continues on. It may seem bizarre that it takes me this long even to mention these gods who, to some, are the only kind of god there is. Those of the British and Irish pantheons are, in a few quarters of the tradition, at the very heart of Druidry, giving it its purpose, structure and focus.

I hope that outlining my theology of deity within Druidry, gods of nature and human nature, has gone to explain my perspective on this point. Yet it would not be complete without an understanding of these named gods, for their power is considerable.

These named gods I call ancestral gods. Gods neither of nature nor of human nature, they are in many ways both, for both energies flow through them, and over centuries or often millennia, their extraordinary quality has been their power to integrate the people with their environment. While we might find our own name for the wind that moves through our valley, or the mischief that regularly swirls through a class of young children, and we might even share that name with others, an ancestral god is one whose name has moved through generations. It is this passage through time that has given it a good deal of its particular quality of energy.

Their stories are usually held in mythology, old poetry or local folklore. They are almost always described in human form, though they may be gigantic in size and most certainly have magically superhuman or even supernatural powers. In British mythology, it is often the women who hold those powers, implying a status that is more clearly divine, while the men are often extraordinary but are more akin to heroes than gods. Importantly, both are flawed, showing signs of vulnerability, ability to feel pain, to be changed and to transform from within. Their stories, perpetually retold and ever mutating in the retelling, can reveal truths and guidance that touch the soul deep down, beneath the analysis of our neocortical reason. Badly told, their treasure is easily lost, the tales sounding like little more than the barbaric complexities of surreal relationships.

My guidance to those who ask me about an ancestral god's nature is that they find his (or her) stories, intuitively choosing one if there are many, and rework that story until it sings to them, evoking emotion that pulls the heart and stirs the belly. Only when they are able to tell that tale, provoking others to gasp and cry, can they claim to have any inkling of the god's nature.

In many cases, it helps to realize that these ancestral gods were once gods of nature: the force of a river, a lake, valley or mountain, of sky, wind or stars, waves upon the shore. When a community's connection with a power of nature is profound over many generations and amplified by a collective social vision, and when that power is named and its effect on the people is deeply respected if not understood, individuals from that community are likely to take with them their inherent honour of that power when they leave that place. They continue to honour, say, the mountain that stood over them, still feeling its energy within their souls. As time passes, memories of the mountain fade and even disappear, yet the name remains, and the effect it had on the people remains – such as a sense of omnipresence, solitude, judgement, paternal harshness and challenge – and the deity of the mountain becomes an ancestral god, perhaps one seen as an all-father, guide and judge.

It is of these ancestral gods that the myths are told. Still holding glimmers of clues as to the force of nature that they originally held, the magical threads connecting the people with their energy run through these tales like invisible wires, shimmering with electricity. If we are able to tap into the flow, they offer glorious vistas of understanding, clarifying what feels like generations of relationship between our heritage and the land. However, too often, the myths and the gods within them are no more than paper money, bank drafts merely symbolic of wealth: the gold that they represent is either lost or inaccessible. Worse still, many are content to celebrate the fluttering of the paper, with no concept of the depth of experience that is the bullion beneath.

There is also an issue around possessiveness when working with named ancestral gods, one that creeps onto the edges of politics and often meanders into brawls. There are people who claim to have the truth about a deity, to know where the god comes from, and resent anyone else who may pose ideas or claim access. It's an issue well known in traditions based on written words, as seekers claim validity for their own interpretations, but it is less common in an oral tradition and, indeed, has even less basis for validity. Disputes on these issues are best avoided, for those raising swords are seldom appeased.

It was brought to my attention a while ago that one person, who was well known in Druidry for his antagonistic and challenging attitudes, was tearing me apart on the ever-peculiar soil of an Internet discussion board. It had been declared that I worked primarily with the Welsh goddess Cerridwen, and he had thrown down a dismissive sword implying my ignorance and dishonour, his doubt about whether I had ever even been to Lyn Tegid. In truth, I acknowledge this person's work, for such sprites of mischief can be useful within any spirituality or philosophy, and I laughed with appreciation when his slander was brought to me. Working with Cerridwen on the shores of her lake – exploring the valleys of her waning slip of moon, seeking her out in the wet darkness of the night – has allowed me to develop a relationship with her; but my connection with that landscape is not strong enough for me to be able to access the ecstatic level of relationship that I would want ... My primary goddess is the power of nature that fills with darkness the valley of my own home.

---

*The words rise through me, as they have done so many times before, her presence behind me, her long fingers upon my spine like melting ice, reminding me yet without thoughts, her breathless breath on the back of my neck. I can feel her looking through my eyes, her soul exploring the energy of each person in the room, gathered as they are to hear her tale, looking up at me, listening, watching my every move, infused with her.*

*And when I pause, she turns to face me, the dark smile of her empty mouth opening, sparkling with anticipation, as if supping on each soul's attention, loving every word I let slide into the quiet of the room, the hearth fire behind me crackling, giving the only light, setting my form into a black silhouette.*

*'. . . and at the end of each day she returned to her cave, to the fire still stoked by that blind old man, to the cauldron set upon it, stirred as it was by that innocent young boy she had stolen from the village, and into that black pot did the witch drop her day's gatherings, those herbs, roots and flowers, each one cut with magic, each one adding to that brew which would give her ghastly son the inspiration of the gods . . .'*

*I feel her fingers slip through my hair, gleeful and cold, and her*
*energy excites me. I know that when the tale is done, the offerings*
*made, and I leave this hearth to walk through the night to find my*
*own, the darkness in the lane will whisper all around me, moving*
*through the trees, awash around my footsteps. And I'll feel that*
*urge to laugh, wild, belly-shaking laughter, like a deluge of rain*
*falling on a wide, slow river . . . And she dances round me,* tell
them, tell them, *and my hands move like the wings of an old*
*raven stretching, like a spirit emerging, disappearing, like a bat in*
*the darkness, as my words keep falling into the air.*

*'. . . and whether it was the mistaken judgement of a blind*
*man feeding a fire, or if it is simply in the nature of a brew so*
*rich with power, but that great cauldron grew hotter, its contents*
*spitting and bubbling as if finding its own life . . .'*

---

When honouring a deity in Pagan Druidry, we are not seeking to
use its power. Awake and willing to feel the awe of perceiving its
spirit, our quest is to understand the *momentum* of its power: the
essence of its intention. Reaching to hear its soul song, our task is
to adjust our own receptors to that same pitch, so enabling us to
journey more smoothly on the currents of its energy when it
gushes through us, beneath us, around us, or indeed to seek it out
if ever we should wish to feel it again.

It is worth noting, and accepting, that we can't choose to work
with a god. We may well like the idea of a glamour puss like
Aphrodite or an independent madam like Bridget, the wild nature
of thunder, the source spring of an important river, or the socially
valuable power of healing, but *deciding* to work with them simply
doesn't work. We are only able to create effective relationships with
those whose energy is already reflected within us. It is said that the
gods choose us: when a part of our own soul wakes, or is woken
by a quirk or trauma of life, that aspect of ourselves is flung wide
open, reaching out into that force beyond our own soul. Given the
opportunity, we can then choose whether to take it or not.

When we do, respect is crucial. We need to consider the ethics and risks of tapping into such powerful drives of energy, be careful not to anthropomorphize and ensure we don't underestimate the force or our lack of understanding. Even gods of human nature are devoid of the rationale of human morality, after all. Remembering that these powers are not always constructive, that each contains its own shadow energy, its dark and unknowable side, we do well too to learn the positivity of the destructive. There are safeguards, but at times it can seem like madness to open our nemeton, revealing our soul-naked vulnerability, and dive into the energy of such powers as grief or rage.

Once again, we can see why it is that the old traditions like Druidry have been feared. From a superstitious standpoint, if a priest is seen to heal a poisoned child, predict a storm, evoke laughter between adversaries or clear the skies of cloud, her powers may seem daunting; but if she is seen to explore and express emotion beyond the wisdom of society, if she can show anger like a tempest or weep like snow at dusk, *by choice*, if she can giggle like a mountain river with no apparent cause, if she can be as still as an old hawthorn in the midst of another's storm, then she is a dangerous creature. Surely there are energies we should not access? The Druid, however, sees none; finding the stillness of balance in the centre of her circle, she reaches out to her edges, discovering life, and learning how to identify these currents of energy, ride them and dive in deep, knowing always the journey back from the edge to the centre's stillness.

Needless to say, how this is done cannot be taught with written words. Yet I would give ideas, returning to the vision of release into the dripping cool and delicious energy of the rain. Waking to its spirit, allowing our consciousness to be perfectly attentive to the rain, our awareness of self dissolves and our nemeton opens completely, leaving only the reality of rain, our mind dancing free and alive within it. We can intensify the experience by first becoming utterly aware of our own spirit and our own flowing energy, so that with heightened consciousness we perceive the spirit of the rain more clearly. If we were to focus on the interaction, on the touch, rain on skin, the point of meeting, soul to soul, body to body, and dissolve into that, we would have yet another powerful experience with a god of nature.

To do the same with a god of human nature like love takes a great deal of trust. It is a sad truth that few human beings ever find the strength and confidence to release so completely into love. When it happens as a gift from the gods, we feel amazed, overwhelmed, truly blessed, but such blessings are most often short and sweet, fading or exploding, and leaving us wondering when or if it will ever happen again. The Druid learns how to do it by choice, in just the same way that he learns how to release into rain.

Instead of suppressing the emotions of rage, lust, grief and fear, Druidry teaches us how to identify the energy clearly, accurately, immediately it touches us. For though at times it is obvious, there are undercurrents of such emotions that flow through our lives, diverting us, distracting us, sabotaging our endeavours with insecurities and instability, with a lack of confidence or commitment. Very often these undercurrents are so familiar to us that we have even forgotten they exist, accepting them as a part of life's normal irritation and frustration, while others accept us as naturally antagonistic, cynical, reticent and so on.

Once we're aware of what the energy is, we learn to hold it, to be conscious of it, not letting that force flood us without consent. We are not suppressing a natural energy, or taming human nature with intellect or analysis, but understanding that what touches us is a thread of something very much bigger: a power of nature. Without this awareness, these emotions can feel horrendously overwhelming. Indeed, if we let go of our defences and are flooded with the emotion, we can be submerged by that power out of proportion to the event that evoked it.

Acknowledging the gods instead, we forge relationships with these forces – both those we may long for (like love), and those we may hope to avoid (like grief). Whether reaching for them or learning how to acknowledge their presence, we come to master the craft of rafting the currents of their power.

# Chapter Seven

# Letting Go: Drums, drugs and screaming

Anyone coming to Druidry to seek information and inspiration about the tradition will encounter those for whom this is a spirituality of the intellect. Beginning with the study of archaeology, of Bronze and Iron Age cultures, of Roman history, the writings of Caesar, Tacitus and Pliny, the student can go on to immerse himself in medieval mythologies and philosophies, ideally learning Welsh, Manx or Gaelic, and knowing the lineages of Order chiefs, their writings and affiliations, their understanding of magic and metaphysics. Through my training in the Craft, I've spent my time on these lessons, memorizing and cross-referencing, studying theories and pondering debates, and amidst the constant fluttering of papers I did find moments of inspiration: the current of history washing over me, the cool rush of continuity, ancestral stories coming to life with the breath of my curiosity.

Just as we can find inspiration in the divine energies of other valleys, so we also find inspiration in other eras, other moments in time. Yet, though the past is the soil into which we root, establishing stability and drawing deep nourishment, the focus of our practice must be the *here and now*. The craft of Druidry as a living, breathing, ever-evolving spiritual tradition requires attention through focused presence if it is to be of any value in how we live and experience our lives.

It is for this reason that a good deal of the teachings of Druidry are about release: the Craft guides us to let go. Disentangling our soul from the past, we learn to break up the limitations of the mind, abandoning expectations in order that the future might emerge shining through freedom, not crawling out submissively from beneath habit and fear. Untying attachments knotted through insecurity and uncertainty, cutting the need to remain socially acceptable, nice and predictable, we allow ourselves to explore life without inhibition, finding the peace that comes with soul satisfaction. We find the truth of our own wild nature, that which is untouched and untamed, true to self, exploring the creativity of our individuality. And while it is Druidcraft that teaches us how to let go, it is through liberating the wild soul that we find the heart of Druidry, too, the deepest mysteries unfolding and touching us with ecstasy.

In the distant past, it was only the Druid who walked this unchained path. A natural priest of nature, he lived the role because he had no other choice – other than to curl up screaming and die. Through the crises of physical pain, disease, trauma, disability and an imbalance of brain chemicals, he didn't see the world as others did. He didn't have the option of social normalcy or complacency, experiencing reality instead as an excruciating poignance of beauty and pain. Some may suggest that, in spirit, pre-conception, he chose that path; certainly, in accepting this perspective, the individual is accepting full responsibility for his state. Without others to blame, the road can seem clearer, allowing a stronger motivation to live and grow through the pain. My sense is that it is simply the wild chaos of nature that hurls upon one person or another the conditions and resources that create an individual who is unable to blend into the norm of society. The Druid shaman did not blend; he was set aside by nature. He learned his Craft as a way of surviving, understanding and accepting the traumas that had forged his own life, and so being able to guide others.

There are still those who walk this road into Druidry, whose physical or mental state is sufficiently skewed physiologically for them naturally to be thrown upon the path of the priest or seer. Where once life events such as tuberculosis, leprosy, polio, birth or battle trauma caused a person to ride off the rails, nowadays it is more likely to be car crashes, cancers and mental breakdowns that drag people into new visions of reality. Some people, like myself, are born with an illness or disability that provides the requisite crisis. The issue is not how or when it happens, but that the individual is (now) able to perceive the world very differently. This is the *shamanic wound*: an ongoing state of trauma that provokes the mind into the sensitivity needed to see spirit, to hear the songs of existence, to feel the pain of pollution and the sensuality of harmony.

For those who are thrown into it, at first the change can create desperation. The guy ropes and reference points that hold the normal human being stable are torn clean away or suddenly recognized as useless, yet nothing is yet within grasp to replace them, and replacements feel crucial. Slowly, over time and with the hardest lessons gently finding ground like snow settling on the grass of the meadow, that desperation dissolves, the craving for certainty quietly released, and though the seeking continues, still provoked by the pain of that wound, the individual learns to live through a state of calm acceptance. This is the journey of the natural priest whose mind has been broken apart. Finding a constant state of release overcoming pain and limitation, relinquishing the option of clinging to the past, he holds no expectations of the future. His wound disallowing complacency, he is offered instead a vision of total possibility. His disability lays down physical limitations that force his life focus on to matters of spirit, to observing the pathways of the mind, rivers of energy, with each step taken in the *here and now*, for nothing else is true.

There are and always have been some among these wounded people who can carry neither the vision nor the pain. Confused, they find themselves collapsing into mental health crises and medication, or reaching for society's analgesics of alcohol and drugs, high-stress work, cult religions or passive entertainment: highways of escapism that ease the moment, for a while, but are actually untenable for the acutely perceptive mind. Yet when facing the pain without a framework or language that adequately and appropriately supports the soul's strength, too often it is only the weakness that is affirmed, and the individual breaks further, sliding into madness, losing control. If there is anything that can enable him to ignore the problem, he will keep trying to take it, overbalancing to grab it, for society's fear encourages him to do so. Humanity's powers of denial and stubbornness are incredible.

Yet, of those souls who are hurled into the experience of something mind-shattering, of those whose physiology offers an eleventh percentile vision by virtue of either trauma or nature, a handful do find the path of the Druid, the priest of nature, just as they have throughout time immemorial. Here there are words to describe what we see, a shared language that gives terms for energy and sensitivity, for the dead and the drifting, for spirit visions and soul-deep pain. It is a language devoid of dogma, without a hierarchy of authority that disempowers, never judging or demanding allegiance. It welcomes every individual in their quest for understanding, and it listens.

When I came to Druidry in the early 1980s, the majority of accessible or known Druids were intellectuals, analyzing and pondering streams of history and metaphysics. It all seemed to me hopelessly disconnected from the natural world. It was a male-oriented culture and immeasurably dull, supported by books that sent me to sleep with their tedium. There are still some who follow this road, considering the tradition no more than a spiritual philosophy, reaching for ideas to contemplate and debate, while not considering practice. For those who are desperate to find spiritual value and direction, who are thrown into the quest by some soul wound, such attitudes of intellectual pondering are unfathomable.

I thank the gods that it wasn't long before I found those who were profoundly and magically bound to the land, the wild souls whose teachings had persisted through millennia, Druids and natural priests whose religion was that of the rain, the moon, the waves and the wind. It was their language that affirmed my vision, leading me from the brink of life and into the rhythms of its dance.

There are many now, however, who come into the Craft *without* this deep shamanic wound. This is a modern development in Druidry: people come seeking not because their state has driven them to the edge of society or life itself, but simply because they feel dissatisfied with their existence. They have found no happiness in money, superficial relationships or consumerism, and the measures society uses for value or achievement make no sense – while all the time the natural world is increasingly abused for those very causes. Furthermore, for an increasing number of people in modern Western culture, there is time to ponder *why*, and even *what can I do*, and it is these questions that now draw folk into the tradition.

For these whose motivation to explore the tradition is simply a profound feeling of inner dis-ease, that deep soul itch which disallows them from meandering unthinking through society's complacency, Druidic theories of life and death, its intellectualized concepts of history, psychology and culture, are either all that they want (mental satisfaction) . . . or they are worse than useless. It is the craft of living that is of importance when we are doubting and debating how to find value in daily existence. The spiritual practice of Druidry becomes essentially about how to take each step in a sacred manner.

For these people who have not been battered by life to the point where their souls lie open, where their vision is raw and their nemeton is flayed by pain or trauma, there is not an unceasing vulnerability of release. In truth, they have no need to face death nor to be the fool. Their nemeton may be cracked or uncomfortable but, like their lives, it is still functioning. Yet such people constantly land on my doorstep – they are in adequately good health of body and mind, and ask with the urgency of their frustrated dissatisfaction that I guide them to see more, to feel more, to understand more ...

———⟫◆⟪———

*'Can you teach me to see the dead?'*

*Her eyes are bright and wide open, a curl of hair softly delineating her face. It reminds me of my six-year-old nephew, his face round with wonder, asking, 'When will you teach me to ride a broomstick?'*

*I know it's a question she's been wanting to ask me since we sat down to talk. She has a picture of who she could become, a seer, shimmering with the kudos of being deliciously fey, so distinctive, and with such magical powers. It's TV glitter, total fiction, and in this case it's compounded by tales of a grandmother who read cards and talked to fairies, another imaginary role model with just the glamorous side on show.*

*And I smile, but inside I feel sadness. She doesn't understand my reticence and, with her head on one side, adds, 'It's not like I'm starting from scratch. I mean, I can feel energies, and I had this experience in my nana's house ...' and she tells me the story, what it was she was quite sure she'd seen as a child, and how it had scared her, 'but ... I think all I need is to* understand *my powers and then I could use them properly. I mean, you don't get scared, do you?'*

*Again I smile, aware of having said nothing for quite some time, remembering the face of a woman at my car window, the traffic stationary in every direction, a bad accident some way ahead, her face, so battered, streaked up with blood, gasping in terror as she wanders from car to car, failing to realize why no one is taking any notice of her, why no one can see her, until she notices me, notices that I've noticed her, and I breathe in deep and close my eyes as she runs to my window, my car window, and screams, screams with a terror that cuts through me like ice, like a stalactite slow-falling through my spine.*

*'Do you get scared?' She doesn't really want to hear my*

*answer, but she waits wide-eyed.*

*'Sometimes.'*

*Sometimes just very tired.*

*'It's just that I really think with some guidance I could help people . . .' She pushes that lock of hair behind her ear, looking at me earnestly through her twenty-something years.*

*Some seers, I know, have a gentle life, opening their vision only when they want to, when asked to contact some late beloved or survey a house. I know that it may well be possible to clean up this girl's vision, fine tuning her sensitivity so that she can see a little more clearly the flows of energy, of emotion, of a soul's passing by. But I can't help wondering whether if she really knew what was in the box, she would want to open it at all.*

*'Do you really get scared?' she says, frowning. 'When?'*

---

Training in the craft of Druidry is not a case of learning some stories, a little history and philosophy, and of being able to identify some wild flowers and trees. Nor is it possible to develop a deep and useful sensitivity that only works in the countryside with butterflies and bunny rabbits. The process of exploring the Craft, training daily with ongoing commitment, has a powerful and holistic effect. It leads us to see the desolation and decay in sparkling detail. It leads us to question all that we are, no longer allowing denial and compromise where before we could sustain it. Even if our goal is exquisite connection and clarity, a seemingly benign aim, the journey should not be taken lightly, for in many ways learning the Craft naturally breaks up our reality, our old paradigms and compromised relationships, in order to establish something that has an irrefutable integrity. Even for one coming to the tradition from a position of basic frustration and soul dissatisfaction, much is often swept away before the soul's landscape can be resown.

It is not an easy path to take, and how we make the necessary steps is not always clear. However, where layers of habit and protection are strong, freeing ourselves from all that holds us constrained can to some degree be achieved by increasing our sensitivity. The sense of separation, the lack of connection and comfort of belonging, are eased or released by waking our soul to the world within which we live: the wild, tender and transient creativity of nature. Rooting deeply into the earth, reaching out into our sky freedom, as we heighten our ability to touch, taste and smell more acutely, and learn how to listen and so to hear truly, we ground and stretch our physicality into the material world, ever better able to perceive its exquisite nature.

Even though such sensitivity reveals the pain as well as the beauty, feeling more in touch with the world around us has a powerful effect. The soul is eased by the connection. We sit in stillness with the dead body of an owl on the road, we follow the slalom fall of leaves through the colours of autumn; even where any relationship is subconscious, when we are just sitting by the river, closing our eyes into the sunshine, floating into the music, the fact that we are there, being touched by another spirit, makes all the difference. By bringing a clearer awareness to those connections, we gain a more acute sense of our own spirit, which in turn increases our personal confidence and inner strength. Our human need for constant external affirmation or the security of an agreed reality gently fades. Simple connection takes its place: being there, we find acceptance.

As we learn better to acknowledge and perceive soul flows of intention, sensing the idiosyncrasies of nature, we are not only able to read others more easily, but can also more accurately distinguish between ourselves and others: the boundaries become clearer. Yet, with a more reliable consciousness of the nemeton, we can also better blur those edges, and so feel ourselves connecting more deeply, touching and being touched more profoundly.

In some cases, however, even with the inner confidence that comes with establishing soul connections in nature, *just* increasing sensitivity can be counterproductive. There are many people whose protective barricades are raised specifically because the soul is too sensitive to cope with the chaos of life. The nemeton is toughened, self-defending, generating a limited and inhibited expression. The thickened layers of scar tissue and defensive padding are too well established to allow any of the freely flowing inspiration and creativity of sacred relationship. If we are to find any level of true freedom through release, it is necessary to break down these barricades, yet with an understanding that doing so will primarily increase fear, a sense of vulnerability and loss of control. To balance the sensitivity, there must be a synchronous transfer of faith from the externally erected defences to the invulnerable spirit of the core.

The process takes time, often years of profound commitment, with dedicated daily practice and ongoing integration. We focus on meditation and the nemeton, learning more about that powerful sanctuary of the soul, building sacred relationships that feed the essential core of our being with rich awen. We become vigilant as to how we are reacting to the world around us, when we are using our nemeton edges defensively, aggressively, and replacing such reactive behaviour with honourable response.

Realizations come in bursts, exquisite breakthrough moments followed by frustrating periods of no change, as the new perceptions settle into a congruence that flows through the soul into our attitudes and behaviour. Gently we find the freedom to let the wild soul breathe.

I have spoken about the animism of Druidry, about all life being rich with spirit, and each entity expressing its own soul song. I have spoken about my Druidic theology, about the deities, powers of nature within and around us. We have looked at how to root and find nourishment in the earth, and how to extend our being into the formless skies, finding the power and beauty of sacred connection. But how do we achieve these moments? How do we soften the nemeton into a flexible and natural boundary that is relaxed and adaptable, and open to transformation, so that the soul can indeed express its wild truth, and make relationships based on that truth? For without doing this, Druidry remains a theoretical concept, not a living practice.

What holds us contained is fear. The element of our psyche that chatters internally, justifying, rationalizing, critiquing, readily tries to convince us that lowering our defences is not a wise thing to do. Our neocortical self protects the childish limbic self that is so afraid. However, it is the fear that cripples and, if we were to lose that fear while allowing reason to walk with us all the way, life would be very different indeed. But how do we do it?

Primarily, Druidry teaches us to accept fear as a power of nature, a deity. Instead of cowering before this force as if it were an icy gale, we perceive it as a current we can actually step out of. While we must retain a respect for the power of the emotion, it is unnecessary to be overwhelmed by it, submitting to its divine compulsion. Equally, we don't suppress the emotion, keeping it tightly under control in our bellies. Fully facing it at every opportunity, we learn how to recognize when its energy has been evoked within us, and how to neutralize that energy, separating it from both the neocortical justifications and the instinctive perceptions of the fear's cause. We can analyse if we wish to do so, allowing curiosity to explore, but more importantly, a neocortical role is simple acceptance and the ability to step aside, letting that energy dissipate or using it creatively. Where it isn't possible to find shelter from the storm of this god, when we can't extricate ourselves completely, we can through practice learn to walk with it in dignity, coming to understand its currents so as to avoid tripping and falling or going under.

We are only ever afraid of the future, after all. It is not possible to fear the moment in which we are standing. All anxiety is based on what we are anticipating will happen. However, as we let go of the past, acknowledging the value of our experience as contextual and over, so do our expectations of the future melt away. Taking the wisdom gained at every Samhain – when another year is closed with the end of the growing cycle and the past year is actively released – the Druid utilizes this practice too in every other part of her life. As dusk falls, the day ends and prayers are made of letting go with thanks. The process of closure, so evaded by our culture, is clearly taught, focusing on the act of claiming with thanks what has been given, and offering with honour and detachment that gratitude. The flow of regeneration made possible through such release opens out the wealth of potential, and with that comes strength and courage that allows us again to walk away from fear. Life is ever fresh with potential. Nothing is impossible.

The fear of change is also poignant: when we are surviving in the status quo, is there really sufficient value in trying something new that we have no certainty will work? Lowering our protective barriers may be catastrophic – or so it can seem, considering the level of vulnerability the idea can evoke. Yet in teaching us to walk our path in harmony with the cycles and tides of nature's ever-changing world, so does the tradition ease our fear through that same landscape. Nothing is permanent. In such a changing world, we can never take the same walk twice; we can never step again into the same river, for the waters keep moving on.

Furthermore, we can learn better to use the exceptional ability of our human nature to adapt, and to do so consciously. It is incredible what we are able to accept, continuing our lives in situations of trauma, scarcity, war and disability. Yet none of this is possible if we are immobilized by fear. Releasing ourselves into the present does not imply resignation or submission, but acceptance: allowing the future to be what it will be. A situation may not turn out OK, and it may not get easier than it is now, but ensuring that each footstep is placed with integrity and honour, we live and work with as much clarity as we can grasp, *here and now*, conscious of our choices, preparing our path with vision and respect, while accepting, too, that nature is wild. Anything might happen.

The fear of rejection is also evident in this process of releasing the soul. If we were to let go of our constraints and express who we truly are, the sense of risk is tremendous; to be disliked, either personally or in terms of our creativity, is much easier to bear when what we are presenting are half-truths. Yet our truth is usually far more clearly perceived by others than we imagine, even through the slats of our defensive barricades, through our hiding, glamours and deceits. We shall never find peace or satisfaction until we allow our soul creativity to be expressed. Furthermore, Druidry guides us to realize that we are never alone, but ever connected across the web of spirit, to which our consciousness slowly awakes. Rejection may mean changing the company we keep, or changing ourselves; either way, stepping with responsibility, we are more likely to find peace.

Rooted in the earth and through time, breathing the beauty of the skies, like a tree we learn to feel centred in our growing self-expression. Yet here we also seek out a third element: fire. This element is wild energy that cannot easily be tamed or contained. In Druidry we find within it the energy of courage, and like most wells of inspiration, it is in relationships that we source fire. Fire meets fire in a way that is unique, for two flames brought together become one flame, no bigger than one alone, seeking fuel and oxygen in just the same way. Stepping a little closer together, sharing the energy of life completely, fire teaches us trust; as our soul songs come together, the fires of spirit bring us strength and confidence, giving us the courage to trust more deeply, so finding another level of freedom, unchained.

Understandings and realizations about the nature of our fear may help us to release it but, as I have said before, Druidry doesn't require a deep level of analysis. Indeed, it is often when we *don't* consult our thinking self that we are able to release the fear. Whether our aim is as basic as to live through another night or, wrapped in the complexities of culture, to succeed at an event without being sabotaged by fear, the importance of holding a clear intention is paramount; when fear is provoked in the limbic brain, we accept its flow, and we either step aside, or use the energy, ever focused on our intention. In learning Druidcraft, it can be powerful to follow this course on purpose, choosing an intention for creative energy, then allowing fear to be evoked specifically in order to find the path through. This kind of cathartic process not only helps to clear the backlog of emotional energy suppressed in the soul, but also connects us into the wider human consciousness of fear, encouraging us into deeper relationship with this divine force of nature, and leaving us with a more profound and holistic sense of release.

In provoking fear, we often find anger rising, for it is often with anger that we bury our fear or cope with it. Sometimes when addressing fear we find grief, intense and seemingly infinite wells of inexplicable sadness: the desperation of losing what our fear is holding on to. We can find shame, that inversion of fear, which is so fundamentally self-negating. Guilt, too, pushes through, with its own waves of energy, and it is so often an expression of our failure to use anger well; we turn its sword upon ourselves. It can be frightening to let these emotions emerge into the light, revealing or experiencing such depths of personal and universal pain. Yet Druidry offers its temple sanctuaries. Guiding us to create moments in time and space, with a few minutes of ritual at its simplest or through hours of elaborate ceremonial, we establish an environment of safety specifically to explore these edges of our soul. Within that sanctified moment, we nurture our relationship with the ruling forces of these wild emotions, and with the powers that teach us along the way.

---

*As if a hand had been placed on my shoulder, I find myself back in the forest grove, feeling strangely as if I've woken although I've not been sleeping. I look up from where I am crouching, as if stretching my eyelids, blinking. The fire is small but bright, flickering yellow and gold in the darkness. The other two women are swaying, their eyes closed, their souls swaying with them, out of kilter with their bodies, blurring their forms with washes of soft colour, indigo, purple, russet, deep green.*

*A burr rises in my throat and I realize I've coughed myself out of trance, retching with the energy of the journey ricocheting through my physical body. Exhausted and shaking on the muddy ground, I wait, wrapped in patience and stiff muscles, knowing that through the fog of my mind the rite's intent will emerge again. Around us, so distinctly, I can feel the bounds of our circle, cast securely to hold us undisturbed, blessed and shimmering with the forest undergrowth, holly, hazel and thorn. What is beyond* the grove barely seems to exist but in a dream, and what is within feels part of my own soul.

One of the others' voices rises from a mumble into a cry of sudden fear and I look up; her soul flitters on blackbird's wings, nervous, waiting, worry trembling through her subconscious mind, for I've fallen through the veils away from her. I breathe down into the ground, feeling the mud energy rising into my limbs, through my blood, preparing to let go, to break out of my mind once again.

I start with our bonding word, the invocation in sound that holds us together, the word that draws us from the disparate journeys of our own soul adventures, an ancient language whispered, again and again. And as the word starts to tumble through me like a stream through a watermill, I remember why we are here: the image of our shared intention fills my mind, this quest for clarity about the land around us, this why? ache for understanding. And hearing my call for unity, returning to the fire, the blackbird and the vixen sliding into their human bodies, they offer their voices like soft water into the cauldron of our intention. Sharing the invocation of this moment, our voices tumble, one over another, rising in the darkness through the trees, finding strength and glory like a storm, lifted by the wild wind into screams of diving-gliding freedom, then pouring down over a great river, the cold, dark fluidity of the sound falling, cascading down into that bottomless cauldron.

Very quickly, the vixen is gone again, following the sound, sliding on its sparkling current down into the depths, leaving trails of energy behind her. My body is in too much pain, and again and again I am distracted from the darkness of the well, sliding instead into the gashes torn across my flesh by pain. The blackbird hovers around me nervously as I start to retch again, my soul pulling away from my physicality; she finds it harder to let go and I am giving her an excuse to stay in control. Across the fire I throw a heavy wildcat paw, claws outstretched, and catch her human flesh, hearing her fear break into anger and indignation, and she rises up on her wings and releases, diving up into the

*dark flow, chased by this cat skidding as if on black skates of oil.*
*And the chant is lost again, as voices slide into the dark behind*
*us, and before me the visions rise.*

⟾◆⟽

In Druid ritual, chanting is an effective way of breaking up neocortical control, allowing us to see reality in totally different ways. Sometimes it is as if the chant numbs the talking self into a stupor, encouraging our consciousness to find stimulus elsewhere, which is why chants need to be so simple that they require no thought. Words or sounds that are symbolic, holding deeper layers of meaning within them, can be powerfully used, for they push the mind into spatial modes, away from logic and verbal reasoning. The chants I use are usually made up in the moment, then forgotten, or invocations of words sacred to me, such as names of gods I am working with.

The uninhibited scream of the young child is something that we lose too easily, the admonishments about inappropriate or disruptive behaviour removing our ability to let go at will. Yet screaming is a potent force. Shattering the air around us, it opens out potential, while within our own souls the act of expressing ourselves with such vocal violence naturally breaks down barriers. Of course, without any integration of change, those walls will rise up again, but where the expression is consciously made, new patterns of energy can be affirmed and settle.

Even without yelling at full volume, vocalizing can smash useless and restricting fears and pride, waking our hearing to a higher sensitivity and respect. Emoting through sound breaks up limiting paradigms, letting our voice fill the air, expressing the poignance and tides of our own wordless songs within the moment. Grief, fear, pain and anger, all act as currents within our souls, and to sing with these gods of nature is to find a way of journeying with them: surfing instead of sinking. Indeed, their songs are usually better told in screams than breeze-ditties.

Drums, too, are often used, saturating our attention and allowing the mind to wander more freely. I find it hard to remain in a deep state for more than fifteen minutes or so while drumming myself, for my body cries out with resistance, but a beautiful priest I worked with for many years often used to drum us through ritual, allowing me an unremitting rhythm on which I could journey undistracted, and giving himself the focus, together with the not inconsiderable physical exertion and pain, both of which facilitated his own soul travelling. His hands would regularly bleed over the goatskin of his drum, having beaten the rhythm of our rite for what felt like hours without end.

Using different drums, with different vibrational pitches, can take us in different ways. The wide earth drums with low tones draw the mind down into the mud and stones, while other pitches resonate with energy centres in our human bodies, such as the sexual vortex at the base of our spine, the low belly or the solar plexus. As those who create dance music know, a heart-pitched drum can adjust our pulse completely. Drums the size of a human skull, well pitched, can shift the vibrations that move through our brains to powerful effect, and not always comfortably. It is worth playing with different drums and rhythms, listening to music close and loud, identifying the pitches that resonate through the body and what they feel like.

Many choose dance as a key ritual tool, or indeed find themselves compelled to dance though they may not understand why – whether the rhythms they hear are in music around them or sourced somewhere within. It isn't simply celebration or sexual play that inspires us to dance; there is a pulse in nature that we begin to hear more clearly as our Craft skills of listening heighten, a pulse that urges us to move. It isn't only our own heart rate, for that pulse is in the vibrations of life around us, in the wind, the land, waterways and rain, in the sap of trees and the breaking of clouds, everywhere.

In Craft, it is also in honouring the importance of our physicality that we dance, celebrating our bodies as an expression of our creativity. As we (metaphorically) undress, removing the constraints of inhibition, unbuttoning and letting fall our fears that we might look foolish, finding the sensuality of our curving, soft physical form, we loosen up our vision of self. If we are dancing within a ritual space, held by the sanctuary of a nemeton temple, driven by an intention and persistent rhythms that veil our exhaustion, we might continue to dance for long periods of time, and the shift in our consciousness can be significant. Releasing chemicals that course through our veins, the dance leaves us feeling high. Letting the corsets drop away, the wild soul finds its body, and moves freely.

Pain is another way of altering consciousness. While the natural priest may live with it as a perpetual provocation of release, those who seek a way of opening the mind can use its magical energy by choice. Numerous tribal cultures have rites of initiation, rites of prophecy and rites that mark the passage of the seasons that include feats of enduring pain. Using tattooing, scarification, piercing or fire, the chosen individuals or priests loosen the mind, opening their vision to what expectation and habituation would otherwise smother.

Surrendering to the pain, letting go of control, and so affirming consent, we take more fully the responsibility of choice, allowing this divine force of nature to seep through our bodies, evoking chemical responses, flooding us with instinctive reactions that must be held with care if we are to use the pain most effectively. For example, the very idea that we might want to experience the pain of a tattoo is counter to our natural reaction to make the pain stop, yet to welcome it, opening ourselves in acceptance, creates a profound conflict in the mind that must be overcome; it is breaking through this conflict that allows the poignance of release.

Written accounts of the Druid tradition describe sensory deprivation and rituals involving the facing of fears, death and madness, and some of those in modern Druidry continue to use these techniques, together with consensual pain through ritual tattooing and more intimate exchange. Fasting also shifts brain chemicals, initially from the weakness of having no energy input, but also through the releasing of stored toxins in the body as fat then muscle are broken down. None of these actions is easy, completely safe or sensible, but neither is the wild soul. The effects and effectiveness of any journey vary according to the individual, body and soul, their spiritual guidance and the intensity of the chosen process.

Toxins are, of course, also used to facilitate release.

In Druidry, as in any serious nature-based spirituality, things that powerfully affect or alter our perceptions are considered sacred, and thus are not used without true respect. Alcohol, plants and fungi, drugs gathered, concocted and brewed, are potent forces of nature. We don't use them for escapism, to reinforce apathy or enhance aggression. They are not recreational. That isn't to say that they are not used; they are. Attitude and intention, however, are keenly wrought.

Celebration is an important part of the old traditions, for where life is acknowledged openly as being bloody hard, so are the good times unequivocally proclaimed. The joy of gathering together is always profoundly acknowledged and celebrated, as are the eight annual festivals, each one marking the turning cycles of the year through growth, achievement, process and release, our paths of learning, giving and receiving. Furthermore, whenever a ritual includes vows sworn, a prayer or intention declared, the rite is always affirmed to have been done – completed with honour and witnessed – while still within sacred space, with the ceremonial sharing of bread and alcohol.

Traditionally in Druidry the alcohol is mead, the oldest alcohol found in the British archaeological record, but cider and whisky are more local to some areas or family lines, and so more pertinent to the rite and those who have gathered. Both are blessed: the bread as a staple food, and the alcohol as a liquid fire that warms the belly (in times past, it was often safer to drink than water); the land and the sun are honoured for the gifts of nourishment provided. Certainly, both historically and even now, the gathered community may get drunk and witless, alleviating the stress of everyday life as people have done throughout time; the priest does not.

Alcohol, herbs, fungi and other poisons have been used for clear purpose throughout the evolution of human spirituality. Cannabis has been used for many millennia, hallucinogenic mushrooms are no new human invention, and our countryside is rich with other natural toxins of various strengths, from mugwort to henbane to fly agaric. Each one holds a different potency, creating different effects in the body and mind, from an increase in general sensitivity, trust and openness, to the smashing of the mind against the granite rock face of death. Furthermore, every landscape has always had its own sources of these natural toxins, and priests have always known and used them, imbibing or ingesting the drug for the specific purpose of getting seriously and sufficiently stoned to loosen their perception of the world, in just the way they chose.

And drugs do break up the mind. Acting across the broadest range of potencies, the plants' chemicals alter the natural balances, potentially tearing down those barricades that keep us constrained, limited and chained. As is the case with pain, our ability to surrender into this process of release to some extent guides just how far it will take us out of the boxes of our safe reality, and into worlds of entirely new perception. For a number of reasons, however, Druidry does not encourage the use of drugs.

I have experienced and witnessed others taking exceptionally dangerous concoctions, and I have heard plenty of anecdotes to add to the pile: responding to merciless emetics, liquidating and ejecting the contents of the stomach and bowels, it feels as if the body and soul are literally being turned inside out. Barely conscious of any reality at all as the poison kicks in, the process makes us stagger from that place of physical depletion into a period of visions, before we pass out completely. Without training (and even with it at times), it is luck whether or not the visions come before the coma-like sleep. More importantly, although memories of the experience may stay with us, there is no assurance that whatever is seen during that period when the mind's casing is in smithereens will ever be integrated and so become useful.

Using chemically processed or constructed drugs would seldom be considered by the natural priest, and this is often as true for those drugs created legally by pharmaceutical companies as it is for those that are marked illegal. The ethics of the licit industry are soiled by issues such as animal testing, dollar-led decisions and pollution, while those of the illegal trade are equally flawed by violence and money. As important to the Druid, however, is the lack of opportunity for relationship with spirit, and this is considered the reason why the effects of such drugs are so harsh, dry and exhausting. A friend once likened it to cyber sex with a computer-generated image: wearing a suit that, wired into the computer, stimulates the body sexually to extraordinary degrees, the experience is utterly without emotional interaction. It is all about release of energy and devoid of the regenerative emotional and spiritual nourishment sourced in relationship.

Yet another reason why the Druid encourages caution when taking drugs is that any substance that clearly shifts the neural chemical balance and alters consciousness is extremely demanding. Whether we are aware of the process as a relationship or not, like the compulsion of a new love affair it takes up the major part of our focus. Completely wrapped up in it, we may believe we are freely responding to others in the world around us, but every other thread of connection is limp. The flow of our energy is wholly internalized or running to the spirit or chemical that has changed our vision. We become selfish: an attitude that is entirely counter to the principles of Druidry.

Of course, with preparation and acute awareness, it is possible to manage this difficult and inevitable aspect. If we are conscious of how the chemical shift alters our nemeton, and awake to what will be needed in terms of connection, we can slide into a sanctuary in order to learn from the relationship while not dishonouring others around us.

With natural sources of toxins, because the tenets and ethics of the Druid tradition are about relationship and not consumption, about equality and not authority, the Craft teaches us how to make ecstatic connection, spirit to spirit, never using another's creativity unnecessarily or without deep respect, never affecting or killing without need and consciousness.

We cannot survive without ingesting food. However, many people in our culture eat in order to ease an emptiness of the soul, confusing food with love, security and affirmation. Yet, when we don't physically need the calories and nutrients, we can find the soul nourishment without eating, through spiritual connection. By taking an apple and holding it in our hand with wakeful sensitivity, we can accept its soul intention, its *eat me* flesh, its *bury me* seeds, its *hold me* stalk, understanding the path that brought it into the present, the energy of apple tree, with soil and sunshine, and touching its spirit our respect grows for it. If we then eat it, the taste is more poignant; but to eat it without need or awareness is dishonourable. It may be sufficient simply to hold it, and share a moment, being together: the relationship is enough to sate our hunger. It may sound implausible, but in the Craft it works.

The same is true of drugs. With a basic ethos that we don't have the right simply to take what we want and use as it as we wish, the Druid's practice reflects her vision of what is necessary and what is not. In other words, it is possible for the Druid to connect through sacred relationship, submerging with consent into the energy of another's soul song sufficiently to feel a physical effect through her own body, without consuming that spirit's manifest form.

When we need a particular kind of response, whether it's tea and hugs or scepticism and laughter, we intuitively call upon the particular friend who will give it. In the same way, when the Druid is questing a certain kind of energy – a stillness, a different sense of perspective, a sharp strength, a playfulness, certainty – he intuitively seeks out the spirit he knows will share that with him: the oak, perhaps, the white clover, the brambles, daisies, stones. It is possible, however, to go deeper than the emotional. For although emotion is clearly energy that moves through us physically, at times we need that energy to make distinct physical changes, altering chemicals in the body.

Thus might the priest find the hawthorn to calm her heart rate into serenity, the willow to alleviate pain or rosemary to clear her mind. Yet she knows she may not need to ingest any of these as herbal remedies. Instead, honouring the tree and entering its nemeton sanctuary with consent and respect, she sits beneath the hawthorn, the rough bark upon her back, and allows herself to slide into the deepest connection she can or needs to achieve. Her soul becomes filled with the song of the tree, of hawthorn-*ishness*, and letting go of all that holds her constrained and limited to her own body, she slips instead into the flow of energy that is the music of the tree. In profound need, she can open her soul so deeply that the awen shared is explosive, breaking the barriers that are creating the problem. Indeed, if she herself doesn't require this specific pitch of energy, once she is familiar with the song the skilled ovatic Druid can hold it within her, passing it to others through her own intention, letting it flow through her fingers like water. This is deep soul healing and yet so gently and simply done.

In terms of drugs that release the mind, the principle of sacred relationship is just as effective. Working with toxic plants, with practice, the Druid learns how to get closer, soul touching soul, tasting the energy, feeling it washing around her, until she is able to dive in completely, surrendering herself into the currents of the other's essence. It's a step-by-step process, for with each experience of surrender, we encounter greater freedom from the mind's structure of beliefs, which in turn eases our next journey of surrender. So does the Druid explore the depths of nature, within herself and around her, through toxins of various potencies, with various effects, such as foxglove, mugwort, yew, larkspur, thornapple and others.

As we establish relationships, it isn't always necessary to go to the creativity or physicality of that spirit in order to feel the energy. We can make that exquisite connection through the web of spirit, reaching out with our soul intention to touch the other through time and space. A 'witness' may be useful, such as a leaf of the tree, a nut or seed, a pebble from that beach, a bone or feather, the energy of which acts as a mnemonic, reminding us of the moment of surrender. I use homeopathy for this purpose, too, sometimes just holding the remedy, sometimes letting it dissolve in my mouth, the tiniest wash of energy triggering the fullness of memory.

Some people say that it is not possible to adjust chemicals in the brain without ingesting a substance, so we can never reach the same place of release when doing it spiritually through sacred relationship. Certainly, without taking something into the body, we can retain a measure of control, a safety net that ensures we never go further than we can cope with. However, no mystical ecstatic tradition is easy; in fact, its practice is definitively accessible to a limited number of people. There will always be many more seeking than those who glimpse where they are going. That does not negate the journey.

It does get easier over time and with committed regular practice, each step making a difference on the way. Indeed, once we have achieved a state of release, that boundless freedom, however we got there, it is easier to find that state again.

———※◆※———

*The sound of the bumblebees fills my ears. Yet each little flower in the meadow around me seems almost as lazy as the bees, languid in summer colour and open abundance. I close my eyes and breathe in the scent of the breeze, affirming my intention to feel more deeply this land, its banks and bumps, stones and paths, all telling their stories of an ancient community. With eyes closed, I simply listen . . . bumblebees and skylarks.*

*There is a song in the grass close by that evokes a glimmer of an old memory. Soft yet clear, it is so deeply familiar that as I turn I half expect to see someone I know walking towards me. But instead, I see a tiny mushroom. Then another, and as I rise on to my elbows I see there is a little scattering of pink-nippled mushrooms, delicate on pale stems, half hidden in the forest of the grass. Rolling onto my belly, I breathe in their scentless softness and smile, and I whisper a* request, sacred spirit, may we share, *hear my song as I hear yours, spirit to spirit, soul to soul, may I dance with you? . . . and almost immediately I hear more clearly the deep base tone and fey tremolo of their song. I open my soul to the music, completely. Lying back in the sunshine, I can feel the tone of my body changing, as if a part of me were reaching, stretching, aching to meet the high note, wading down to find the low note, and I wait, feeling the shift inside, some roof at the back of my head lifting, the taste in my mouth changing.*

*When I open my eyes, for a moment I wonder how long I've been lying there, suddenly doubtful as to whether it's been just a minute or hours. The grass is longer and such a vivid green, and each strand is more separate in its consciousness, its soul speaking, reaching into the breeze. I pull myself up, breathing deeply, and for a long time I watch the village, laid out as it is around me, people to-ing and fro-ing, the spitting of a fire, dogs, laughing children, a goat tethered to a wall. So much music, an endless day, and I watch, endlessly . . .*

*Moving my fingers in the grass, I touch something cool in the warmth of the sunshine and I turn to see a tiny mushroom I'd forgotten was there. When I look up again, the village has disappeared beneath quiet, grass-covered banks.*

———◆———

What it is we actually see in our increased sensitivity is up to each individual to decide. The same is true of where we go, when we have broken up the limitations of the mind and, no longer constrained by beliefs and expectations, we find ourselves in what appear to be entirely different worlds.

As in all of Druidry, there is no consensus needed. What the individual sees, what he experiences, is framed by his own footsteps upon the path. We see through the filters of our unique physiology, our ancestry, our cravings and understanding. We each tell our own story, and we accept each other's.

It is perhaps easier to recognize the value of increasing our basic sensitivity than of opening our minds completely. The simple ability to perceive the world more clearly, waking our senses where before they were dull with habituation and apathy, patently allows us to create better relationships with those around us. Where we can see and hear accurately, we are more likely to interact with congruent respect and relevance. Where we feel no value or advantage in interaction, with more poignant perception we can make appropriate decisions, and where possible and with respect we can walk away. Where there is value, that is felt more profoundly than ever, feeding the soul with what is truly the elixir of life: what the Druid calls awen.

When it comes to seeing, hearing or feeling spirit – energies shimmering, energy currents in flow, threads of the web of connection, vestiges of old emotion or activity, impressions that have slipped through time, and simply more vivid colours – there is really no need to explain this in terms of 'belief in the supernatural'; indeed, the very phrase is devoid of meaning to the Druid, for there is nothing *beyond* nature. Nature is incredible; a century ago, the mainstays of modern high-tech culture would have been seen as demonic magic. To imagine that at the beginning of the twenty-first century, when people are dying in their millions of hunger, war and abuse, we know about nature is both dangerous and farcical hubris.

When we have broken through the mind's shields of safe familiarity, what we are able to experience may be understood by some people as journeys through the deep unconscious or the subconscious mind, or as dream worlds imagined, created by our own files of experience and belief, as symbology painted with the colours of associations. Others feel that it is plausible that we might slip through some quantum crevasse into another time or place; we could find ourselves in a parallel universe, in another dimension, in other worlds completely. To the mind that is open, there is no proof either way. Certainly, I have too often seen what is generally considered impossible to be limited by the current scientific (let alone social) comprehension of nature. Yet finding *fact* here is not the point: what is important is simply that in our visions we find inspiration, new ideas, insights and realizations. What is equally crucial is that these are integrated, that the energy of that inspiration can flow through into true expressions of our soul's creativity.

In Chapter 3 I provided a list of mental states that lead us into meditation. These were curiosity, interest, attention, concentration and meditation. In concentration we are totally focused on the subject, while in meditation we lose our sense of the world around us. When our mind is broken open, we move one step further, into a state of *trance*: here we lose any sense of our self as well.

Without a sense of who or where we are, our soul is released to explore and develop relationships and landscapes that the limitations of fear or reason wouldn't otherwise permit us to investigate. Although afterwards it can be reassuring for others to affirm our new understanding by listening to the process of our adventure, Druidry emphasizes the value of simply telling the tale, guiding us beyond the need for confirmation of our visions.

In trance, our ability to utilize the potential of the limbic brain is heightened; while riding the currents of divine energy, we are more fully held within the experience. Concurrently, trance facilitates a poignant congruence with the base brain, where there is no separation and there are no boundaries, where we are rain and heat and rising wave, undistracted by self-awareness. Intensifying connection, the powerfully integrated self journeys along the path of our higher brain's intention, experiencing completely.

Of course, not all the unchained mind sees or feels is honey and roses. Once again, in Druidry we learn that nature is not here to love us, nurturing and forgiving us our stupidity and selfish mistakes. Where there are fewer boundaries and barricades, we find demons unleashed, too, and the Craft guides us to face these, full on. Some disappear on contact, the act of splashing a spotlight of consciousness upon them causing them to disintegrate into the dust of delusion. This monster we fear is a part of our soul; being intrigued or even aroused by some horror may simply be a part of the way in which we process the world we live in, through dreams and fantasies. Computer games, films, sports, literature, websites, all give us the option to explore this monster's nature; the vast majority of us would not actually want to be near such situations in reality.

Some demons, however, are not imaginary fears. Human nature is aggressive, selfish and proud, and reacts to nature around us, equally fraught as it is with pain, violence and decay. Without constructed self-defending barricades, in the worlds of trance and visions, the free mind strolls up to these spitting, snarling demons with the confidence of the immortal. With respect but without fear, she allows herself to walk through the 'fires of hell', knowing with gentle surety that these are rites of deep cleansing and transformation.

The guidelines, well written in the Craft, emphasize the importance of the nemeton sanctuary, encouraging trance only within a carefully prepared temple space if it is possible, suggesting offerings be made and respect given to those who support us with beauty and power. Perhaps of most importance is the active choice made to embark on the ride, with full responsibility acknowledged and, when the trance journey is done, thorough attention being given to ending the process, separating from its reality and integrating all that was gained back into the here and now.

It is (almost always) our own choice to break out of the box. Even when life in mainstream society has become intolerable, it is our choice to leave the easy safety of that fold, and how far we move from it. Even when nature has given us an advantage in terms of pain or trauma that sets us on the way, it is our choice to use it or not, accepting or evading. Whether we are looking at simply increasing our perception, or exploding the mind's edges into an eleventh per cent vision, what we are dealing with is profound and sometimes violent breakthrough. Nor is our perception easy, for the pain is as heightened as the beauty. It can feel like madness in comparison to social normality, and it can be judged as such by those who hold tightly to society's rules.

A sense of loneliness is not unusual amongst those who live and work within these deep levels of Druidcraft, for it becomes harder to share our lives with those whose experience of life does not include the power of these visions. Our enthusiasm, clarity or excitement is not enough to bridge the gap in understanding. What we experience can feel threatening to others, as they secure and paint their barriers of self-protection again. Furthermore, if we are *living* the attitudes born of intense perception and sacred connection, expressing the ethics of being in a world that is alive with spirit, and especially if we do so without drugs or other tangible tools that can be credited with our 'madness', our freedom can seem magical and outrageous.

The experience of true inner freedom, however, the sense of utter potential and mind-blowing awen, is often too delicious an option to resist.

# Chapter Eight

# Change:
# Magic and the impossible

With increased sensitivity revealing to us not only the wealth of beauty in the world around us, but also the depths of its desolation and decay, and with learning to connect into the web of spirit enabling us to *feel* that pain as well as the joy, it isn't surprising that the Druid's soul is charged with a desire for healing change.

Furthermore, as the process of learning shows us more clearly our own human nature, and how we play with the energies of the gods, how we flinch and we fight, Druidry leads us into the centre of it all: we have no option to deny our part. Instead, we find ourselves in the midst of the experience of life, aware of our own crises, our cravings and complicity. With the barricades of our self-defending gradually dissolving, leaving the strength of spirit shining through, the Druid steps forwards acknowledging her responsibility as a part of the world she lives in, as a part of nature.

The noise was overwhelming. Above the relentless growl of the city, right in front of us the traffic was stopping and starting, car horns yelling frustration, grumbling double-decker buses, sirens in the distance, and the shouting of police as protesters pushed their way onto the busy street, lying down on the tarmac, fake blood and bandages. And on top of it all, the sounds of gunfire, canons, shells exploding, relayed over a battered PA system, splintering the air clear across Whitehall and into Downing Street.

Holding her hand, I had squeezed and whispered into her ear, 'This is not the sound of war.' She'd shaken her head sadly, 'No.' And murmuring prayers to the powers of nature, rooting down into the ground beneath dirty, cold pavements, hand in hand finding that earth-blessed immovable strength, we had started to add to the noise.

No, that was not the sound of war: bullets, bombs. My mind had filled with images, wide eyes, terrified, children screaming, women running for cover, those bombs exploding, tearing apart flimsy houses, guns held in white-clenched fingers, and such a deep and hollow silence somewhere within the shrieks of panic. Tears, as despair kicks away comprehension. And into the mess of civilized working London, we howled those images of despair, of grief still intangible and strangling terror, veiled in black as we were.

Someone even held the microphone of a megaphone between us, so that our voices were amplified, washing through the crowd and government buildings. We hadn't noticed at the time, so lost were we in the grief of our keening.

The sounds of war, wracking our souls.

Usually, when I find myself confused and low about humanity, I sit in the graveyard. Heading into the forest allows me to forget my selfish race, easing my soul as my focus slips into tree wisdom, the stream's tales, the humming of the mud; yet when the despair *is not one that can be put aside, I find serenity amidst the monuments to the dead of my village. But today, with war still blistering my mind, I needed more. I needed this.*

*I look down from where I sit, high on the bank, and I think of Shakespeare and summer magic (. . . where the wild thyme grows . . .). Spread out before me is the district's landfill site. Acres of waste, barely rotting. Tears rise and I let them fall, silently rolling down the cold of my cheeks.*

*Some light strip of plastic, caught in the wind, is flicking a rhythm as it slaps the side of a cardboard box. I think of how much rubbish I set out on the pavement each week, all that can't be recycled that still comes into my home; how much of this ghastly toxic pit is my doing?*

*The shiny, new lightweight wheelchair I have just bought is aluminium. I remember flying so slowly in a four-seater plane over the grey devastation of thousands upon thousands of acres of Amazon rainforest, wiped out, covered with the horror of vast bauxite mines. In the landscape of my memory, I see hillsides exploding.*

*The slap of plastic is driving me crazy. The sound of war.*

---

The sense of needing to do something, of course, doesn't guarantee that we shall have an impact on the state of the world. It is easy to feel insignificant and impotent in the face of such human disasters as war and pollution. Yet in Druidry the understanding is that we *can* each make a difference. We must. The real issue is how.

In the traditional Witchcraft I learned, magic was completely central to the faith. With confidence based upon an understanding of its tenets and ethics, and upon the ability to step into the powerful stream of some chosen deity, the Witch decides what needs to be achieved, wraps that decision into a spell, and forces the change to occur. Whether she is working with a sick child, a stretch of barren land, the hubristic stupidity of politicians, hers is very much a solitary spiritual practice; one Witch makes her choices as to how a little corner of the world should be, reaching for the power she needs and getting the job done alone.

In practice, most who adhere to this branch of Paganism find the ethics of such magical work increasingly slippery; their confidence crumbles as doubt creeps in as to whether or not they can really ever know what is best in any situation. In reality, getting older, finding broader perspectives and gentle acceptance, her reverential spirituality becomes stronger than her willingness to make changes: the simplicity of being becomes her focus.

This issue of change manifested by force of will is emphasized in Wicca, the twentieth-century blend of old Pagan Witchcraft and occultism. Here, as in various other offshoots from mystery schools, the word used is more often *magick*. Like the capital *g* in God, it is an important *k*, for it specifies change that is consciously created. With many attitudes that originate in medieval Christian occultism, magick usually requires one to follow complicated instructions and keep to certain words and forms. Much of its power is based on reams of associations, mnemonics that enable the practitioner to stride with clarity and certainty into powerful currents of energy. It is altogether more of an intellectualized process needing a dedicated mental discipline, where traditional magic can be achieved through a much simpler level of determination and focus. It is this mental discipline that often maintains confidence in a practitioner's convictions, allowing those who walk this path to practise their craft of asserted change for longer.

Druidry, however, has no *k*. I describe the tradition as an ancient magical religion, yet the magic is not its focus: it's the result.

By choosing not to force a course of action, we are certainly not releasing a situation into the hands of *fate*. Currents of nature, after all, will take any situation and carry it, without consideration, to smash it upon rocks or deposit it upon some distant shore. *Fate* is simply a collective term for all the powers of nature that touch a moment in time, including those of our own limbic human nature, the tides of our emotions, fears and cravings. However, instead of seeking the power to fix a problem as we deem fit, the focus of the Druid is upon the quest for an honourable solution.

When a young child looks up and whispers, wide-eyed, 'Do you do *spells?*' my answer is most often the simplicity of a surreptitious wink. The serious response clearly points to a key difference between spiritual traditions: those based on human magick, those that look to an authority and those that quest natural inspiration.

A spell is a stream of words that acts as a container, sculpted out of a situation and crafted with an intention, into which is poured a flood of energy. An incantation, it can hold an invocation of deity or spirit, or simply hold all that is needed to break through the current situation into one that is new. Just saying words is not enough, even in prep school Latin, for unless there is some other force helping, the undercurrents of our own beliefs will be more potent and formative. The mnemonic value of the words is where the power lies, allowing our mind to unlock doors to visions and realities that would otherwise remain closed.

I don't, however, see modern Druidry as a petitionary religion. We don't beseech the gods to grant us favours: this is a practice that requires a belief in listening, caring and omnipresent deities. Where a magickal spell draws the required power into the soul of the practitioner, a petitionary prayer requests that the deity manifest the change that we desire, but in both cases it is very much our self that makes the decision.

In a tradition such as Druidry, the spell is a prayer: a respectful invocation that opens the soul and presents to the gods and spirits of a situation's environment a request for inspiration, so that a solution can be found. The force of the Druid's own energy flows along the clearly delineated paths of that intention.

Honouring the breadth of our human nature, there is no expectation that the solution could or would be found purely by the power of our human intellect. Nor is it sound to rely on an emotional or limbic motivation. Intuition can be of value; it can also be based on defences, misinformation and insecurities, the logical pathways of which are not fully accessible to the conscious mind. All these are self-focused.

The Druid quests his answer by reaching instead into the relationships relevant to the issue in hand. Whom he reaches to is seldom a problem to decide, for a little sensitivity to the threads will reveal those who are screaming taut, those who are limp with low energy, those who are shuddering with pain. Using the tools of sacred connection, soul touching soul, he feels the other's intention, hears the song, and the inspiration requested slides into his own mind. Spirit touching spirit, the energy required is shared.

Sometimes miracles happen; most often it is the dreadfully complicated twists and tangles of everyday life that are gently unravelled, bringing peace and connection to those moments through which we stumble out of harmony. Emerging from the dross of tired habits and expectations, life seems again to be magical. Nature's patterns and tides seem suddenly to be extraordinary once more. We are filled with the wonder that comes with the recognition and realization of potential. We are inspired, and our vision of life itself is magically renewed.

Our intention is critical.

Primarily, the teachings guide and wake us to how exactly we are connected within any given situation, where the threads touch and how, whose energies demand priority and whose need is predominant in that moment. It can be hard to leave our own will outside, particularly when there is fear of loss within us; it takes time to understand just how we can ensure we aren't blindly projecting our own needs upon another soul.

To throw this into a metaphor of life as a journey, our intention is the *driver* of our soul vehicle, and his vision is based on the maps drawn by our beliefs; the vehicle is fuelled by our limbic emotional energy. Our thinking self may do his best to be the one giving directions, but most of the time he is just a passenger, seldom getting his bottom into the driving seat for more than a short stretch.

We can do our utmost to clarify our belief systems, ensuring that our stack of maps is relevant, useful and easy to read. We can always work on improving the communication between everyone in the vehicle, taking time to listen and respond instead of allowing or indeed provoking panic reactions. Yet also, we learn not to try and drive someone else's car.

Having a good driver is essential: our intention must be clear. The more specific it is, the harder it may be to perceive the inspiration that is the little piece of the puzzle that fits as a solution. Sometimes that extra effort is needed. However, sometimes to deal with that much detail is self-defeating. Furthermore, we must not forget that what is left out of an intention is just as important as what is clearly stated.

Where we can, our intention must embrace all possibilities. If we are not willing to be open to any eventuality, closing our mind to potential, we may find no inspiration at all. If we retain underlying beliefs that assume some path to be wrong, our quest may be sabotaged and, as we remain caged and limited, unable to break a barricade to freedom and creativity, the situation remains unresolved. This reaffirms the acceptance that nature is not just or fair in any human sense of the word: beautiful and painful, sometimes the most appropriate and honourable path is not the easiest to walk.

One trick I've not yet mentioned focuses on helping us to find our truth and intention: I call it the Druid's *shed*. A particularly English term, the shed is a rough wooden construction at the end of the garden. Badly lit and chaotic with dust and spiders, it is the hut where we keep tools hung up on hooks, treasure boxes we should sort or throw out and all the projects we are part of the way through completing. It's a place where coffee mugs disappear. In Druidry, the shed is a symbolic yet powerful place.

In most books on Druidry and Paganism, you will find information on the importance of the cardinal directions and their mnemonics and associations. In my previous books I've encouraging readers to build their own catalogue of associations, but usually, in northern hemisphere temperate Western European Druidry, north is earth, winter, night and darkness; east is air, spring, dawn and discovery; south is fire, summer, daytime and action; west is water, harvest/autumn, dusk and release. In the north, we study death, the void, potential and conception, while in the east is emergence and new growth; south teaches us about the fullness of life, and west hurls us into the crises and relief of release and decay. Dividing the circle into four lists provides smaller chunks to remember, facilitating understanding.

It's a wholly modern aspect of Druidry, a mix of global Pagan ideas, occultism and medieval Christian magic. While for many it is a foundational part of Druidic practice, for me its value is in the realms of exploring our own minds, discovering subconscious beliefs and aiding personal transformation. With this in mind, having four corners, I encourage students to construct this segmented circle as if it were a personal magical shed.

We begin by walking around inside it. Alert to every mental, emotional and physical hint of reaction, we journey through the seasons of the year from north's winter around to winter again; we journey through the course of a day, the path of our life, with each cycle settling connections into place. Gently we discover, organize and decorate, drawing out into manifest expression all that lies in our subconscious, carefully placing events, locating lovers, family members, colleagues, animals, trees, herbs, colours, crises, barricades, beauty and hope ... until we have our entire inner world scattered over every shelf and into every corner of our shed.

Holding it all in our imagination takes some practice. The process of transposing it into a piece of artwork can significantly deepen our understanding when we begin. Of course, it changes as we change. We lose things and rediscover them. We can spend long hours of meditation surveying one quarter, learning about ourselves, moving things around. Now and then, reworking it through creative expression updates that shed-vision of who we are.

Integral to the process of clarifying intention, then, is our own exploration and discovery of what we truly want. For as we sift through ideas in our shed, we learn to spot hidden connections and beliefs that are cynical, closed and fearful. Often undercurrents of energy, these will hijack our apparent intention, manifesting instead the failure and negative feedback that we are clearly expecting. Equally, the quality of energy that floods our intention, whether overtly or subversively, is reflected in the character of the inspiration we receive. If our intention is fearful, our quest may well mirror and intensify that; an intention tight with the anger of judgement will perceive judgement in the reply; if we have no real belief that we shall find an answer, it is unlikely that we would notice any answer that is offered.

The shed itself can be used as a forum for change. Finding an area of crisis, we can place it and then seek a source of inspiration somewhere else in the shed. Spreading the shed out upon the grass, on the beach or the carpet, we can walk its paths, making active physical journeys from conception to the moment just after birth, from puberty to when we first made love, from the day of our marriage to the loss of that perfect love, from the start of study to the exam we are about to take (and the celebration of success we are hoping for): the blocking problem and the inspired solution. As in all Druidic practice, this is not necessarily an analytical process. The light of consciousness may pour over logical connections, offering us reasons for behaviour and events, but the magic need not come through our neocortical computer. Simply making the journeys allows us to explore again both consciously and subconsciously what has happened. Instead of being overwhelmed by one crisis, the shed maintains our vision of the whole circle of life. It allows us to choose a different attitude and response to a situation, painting the past with different emotional energy, and releasing it. It allows us to face the future without the shackles of need and expectation.

In deep Druidic practice, the shed is another level of our nemeton, as both healing sanctuary and sacred temple. It offers clarity about the invulnerability of our spirit core, revealing the concentric circles that expand from there to the edges of our world. Our shed helps us to find our own voice, and in it we can sing the power of our experience.

In many ways it is valid to say that we are manifesting our reality with every breath, every thought and action; the power of magick is simply that process drawn into the light of our consciousness, considered and fine-tuned.

By this definition, in Druidic magic, for each act of creativity we are consciously seeking out divine inspiration, ensuring that what we do is blessed. Only if it is in harmony with the ecology of its time and place, the result of our waking to the intricate beauty of nature's patterns in the web of spirit, will something thrive. Only where there is harmony can our involvement, and our investment of energy, be clearly honourable and ethical.

On that basis, we can see how the very proces of taking down the rigid barricades around our soul can in itself be exquisite magic. Life changes completely.

I have spoken of the nemeton as the sanctuary of the soul. As the area we hold defended around our physical and emotional self, this intimate space can in fact be the 'safe' box that confines us, suffocating our creativity. Yet blessed by an acceptance of the sanctity of our spirit, filled with its shining energy, the nemeton can be our own temple to nature. Indeed, what fortifies and invigorates that energy is not retaining its isolation, but the intensity of connection, the inspired flow of awen: spirit touching spirit. Opening this, our haven, can be difficult to do.

The first steps in this aspect of the Craft involve increasing consciousness of the nemeton's edge. Within the concentrated course of a Druid apprenticeship, we can spend a good number of years on the study of edges, both ours and those of others, allowing our sensitivity to be heightened, until our perception is clarified sufficiently for our behaviour to adjust naturally. Gradually it becomes second nature to respond to another soul with conscious deference to their nemeton. Our manner is infused with a deeper expression of respect and a more holistic acceptance of context and circumstance, of beauty and pain.

Only with acute awareness of edges do we take the next step, learning how to move close enough to enable the edges to touch. As a result, when we do touch, edge moving against edge, our senses are so utterly awake to the sensation that the experience is profound. This is not about being sated on hints of intimacy, forgoing the 'real thing' for some contact that is somehow more refined; it is about the dance of spirit. Too easily do we push and pull, taking handfuls of what we think we need. With consciousness of our nemeton moving against another's, the energy hums, shimmering, responding. The merest touch can shoot ecstasy through the soul. Greed dissolves, the need to grasp and hold, to consume and possess disappearing. In the moment of silent stillness that is fully lucid acknowledgement, perfect acceptance, there is powerful magic: its inspiration charges our own spirit with the fuel of recognition, and upon that revitalized current we ride the white water of change.

We are almost ready to open, yet before we even try, the importance of consent needs to be taken into consideration. Opening our own soul to someone who does not open to us can occasionally be of value, as mentioned in Chapter 4: using our nemeton, we can hold a soul shaking with uncertainty. However, even where someone is in trouble, it can be disrespectful if done without consent, smothering and constraining. Similarly, to enter without invitation where another's nemeton is open, whether we ourselves are open or closed, can be profoundly invasive, even abusive. Establishing consent is essential, and that seldom means spoken or written agreements signed in English. Without skill in the craft of listening, we are liable to make further mistakes; we must be confident in our ability both to ask the appropriate questions and accurately to discern the answer, and often that must be done in the language of the soul, the music of the song.

Some spirits are never closed to us, and in Druidry this can be used as a definition of deity. The sun and earth are obvious examples: we live and breathe within their nemeton or temple space. The water cycle is another example, filling every part of our lives, even when we live far from the coast, so drawing rain, clouds and seas into the category of deity. Of course, to open our nemeton to a spirit whose creativity is so vast, so little concerned with humanity, yet whose essence is a crucial part of our being alive, can be extremely powerful. This isn't about two-way trust but about our human insignificance. The energy can flood through our soul like water through a cracking dam, inspiring, invigorating, yet at the same time it is potentially brutal and dangerously overwhelming. Importantly, and because of the force of this power, even with a spirit or deity whose temple is never closed to us, we must affirm a level of consent. For our minds are generally asleep to this essential energy of our living and, in our quest for that consent, we are both waking our soul and making a prayer that respect be shared, preparing ourselves for what we are about to do. Without such prayers, we risk the hubris of believing we are strong enough to face the power unveiled.

With consent affirmed, we learn by using our fingertips to sense the pressure that shows us the edge. Finding the layer that we will open, we make our decision, for the process will be as effective as the strength of our intention. Then slowly, with acute awareness, we draw our hands apart, leaving an opening in the temple boundary, a gap or open door through which streams of energy can flow, in and out. The craft of closing it is as simple as letting our fingers follow the strength of our intention. For the inhibited, the physical action may seem awkward, but it is nonetheless useful, prodding every part of our psyche into being involved in the process, and giving us a clear visual anchor we can use to remember. Once we've felt the effect and can easily recreate it, pure intention can take over. In time, we can fully open or effectively close our temple doors in the blink of an eye.

Just as happens at the end of any ritual where we have scribed the limits of our temple around us by casting a circle, when we open the circle our intentions in prayers and spells flow out into the web of spirit to make their impact on our worlds. Truth pours out and truth flows in. The effect is magic. Our vision intensifies. We see more clearly the energies of spirit, the currents of each soul, the song of the worlds in which we live. Vivid and intensely alive, we become aware of the threads of the web, and how each soul is connected – ourselves included. We see how every thought and movement shimmers those threads, provoking pain, inspiring beauty: creating change. It is glorious, powerful, horrifying, amazing, invigorating and exhausting.

Within a specific relationship, with consent, as we open so do they, and for as long as our trust is maintained, our two soul sanctuaries are one. The rest of the world disappears. In those moments, we share the most exquisitely sacred space. As the energy flows between us, fear is released. Radiant with trust, the dark depths of potential are revealed. Everything is possible.

Like so much of Druidry, what we are doing is taking a natural act (sharing intimacy) out of the realms of subconscious and intuitive behaviour and placing it into the toolbox for living consciously, creatively and honourably. Powerful intimate connections do break over us now and then, out of the blue, bringing with them exquisite inspiration, profound teachings and realizations, together with feelings like love, respect and confidence; Druidry shows us how it is possible to initiate and create such moments of deep soul-to-soul connection, within every part of our world. This is magic, for by doing so we bring into our communities and our environment the kind of interaction that is intrinsically respectful, mutually nourishing and naturally sustainable. We no long live with complicity in the abusive competition of authority-based society.

Opening the nemeton can be controlled. We can create a chink and peek out. In deeper Druidry, the Craft guides us to open our sanctuary completely: it is a profound act of release into trusting the sanctity of spirit and riding the music of nature's song. In our own space, bounded by the extent of our mortality and creativity, we can acknowledge the beauty of the world around us; opening ourselves fully, the universe becomes our temple, limited only by the edges of our ability to perceive or imagine. There is no safety, and no threat, no beginnings and no ends. There is only the moment, which is infinite.

Our own nemeton is like a boat, drifting upon a lake. With sensitivity we learn how to move with its waves, perhaps rowing in some direction or other. With our seeking we let our fingers slide through the dark water, savouring the softness of its energy. For some there comes a moment when the temptation is greater than the fear and, leaving clothes behind in a heap on the damp wood, they slip over the edge and into the water. Some say the notion of the boat disappears at death, but my sense is that it remains, holding together the cohesion of our soul, until the day our soul song dissipates into the music of universe.

———◆———

*There is no purpose. I'm not here to sort some issue. I am just here. And I close my eyes, resting my head against the hazel bark. At the edge of the forest I made prayers . . .* as I open in trust, I ask that you may accept me in trust . . . *and walking along the old paths and down the badger tracks I've felt free and alive, soul-naked in this vibrance of colour and life. But when I sat down by this hazel on the verge of a field, I was distracted by thoughts. I can feel the bark against my head.*

*I breathe in and whisper aloud, 'Thank you for your support in my thoughtfulness . . . ' the sound fading like a trail through the undergrowth.* Accept my trust, *I murmur.* May we share this moment . . .

*And the bark against my head softens, the edges blurring as I feel myself lighten, the energy of the tree extending around me, the scent filling my lungs. Its embrace is so complete that I find myself sliding back through that smooth and deep brown bark into the wood itself. The currents of energy are steady and I rise up through the trunk, finding myself in twigs, in the wrinkles of bark, out into the sunlit leaves, flushed with deep green and gold, yet at the same time I am fully aware of the cool darkness of mud all around me, damp and holding. For an instant the sense of being conscious of so many different impressions at the same time cuts a pain of tension clean through me; I let go of any need to understand, and drift again into feeling. I feel young and strong, yet ageless, and as a flurry of wind moves a leaf towards me, strangely, I'm not sure if I am that leaf, too. The uncertainty allows my mind to diffuse further, and I find I am conscious of hazel and of nothing else. The mud, sunlight, the shush of the wind, are a part of my hazel-ishness, the song of my soul community, and all I hear is that song, gently as I sing, of leaf and sap and flickering light.*

*A rook, landing on a branch just above me, calls,* I'm down here. *The noise breaks the air, shocking me, and in a split second my mind is gathered up. In a softer* Craa-aw, *his head at a tilt, he adds,* Now what's down here ... *and watches me, listening to the tree songs in the silence. I have no language to ask, but what is needed is spoken, and when he lifts from the hazel to fly through the beech above, rising up through the canopy and into the sky, I am with him, held utterly within the rhythm of wings and breath. There is space all about me, endless, formless space, and this is my breath. And dissolving, I breathe ...*

*Amongst the chunks of stone, pebbles and dry mud, I set my feet, feeling some dusty sensation of form, of a moment's solidity, and without thoughts I take a step or two closer to the still figure beneath the tree. Limp, she looks tired. Her song is dry, a soft reflection of the village noise in the valley below.*

⟫◆⟪

Magic is not just in the breakthrough. It isn't only the wild screaming of breaking up the mind, the crashing out of our box of expectations, nor even about what happens when we have opened our nemeton and danced through the exquisite beauty of that vibrant perception. Druid magic is also about what we do next. It is about integrating into every step upon our path the visions and realizations found in that state of release. How do we *live* its wisdom, allowing that power to affect our every interaction, underlying each thought and word? How do we pour its energy into the magic of all we create? How do we use the perception within the breathing of our daily lives?

I have spoken about the nature of the magic of the bard. Having learned to place her feet firmly upon the ground in presence, she learns how to listen, questing inspiration in the songs and the stories of her community, of her ancestors, hovering in time, the songs that hum through every part of nature. With her sense of self sufficiently clear, conscious of her own soul music, that inspiration flows through her as she shares its magic in her creativity. With finely tuned tools of resonance, using her voice and instruments, using words and sound, she creates magical change, shifting energies, emotions, beliefs and even memories.

The ovate within the Druid tradition is one who perceives the song as colour, finding her inspiration in the beauty and pain of all she sees, currents of energy, waves of vibration, shimmering and pulsing, emerging and decaying. Her magical craft is her ability to discern the paths of these threads of colour, their course through the shadows of the past, and their potential in the darkness and dreams of the future. So does her creativity bring change and healing, within the power of the *here and now*, adjusting hues and shades as she paints a poignance of clarity upon the moment. For simply by clearly seeing what is present, drawing it into consciousness, beliefs rise up to the surface and, fully grasped, can be changed. Where there is struggle, muddy stagnancy, she can use the energy of her own colours to alter those around her, washing a different vibration through the moment, allowing the magic of a new reality to be felt.

Once we have learned how to hear the song, and to see the pathways of the soul, we are ready to step forwards to learn the craft of the Druid, for this is a magic that moves in the very threads of connection. The Druid walks where others watch and listen.

The Druid is the priest of the tradition; her role is to serve, but *what* she serves is for her to decide. She may be concerned purely with the forest, the stars, the oceans. Her forum of connection may be with beetles or eagles. She may work within any part of the human community. She pours her energy into striving on behalf of the sacred, through her own relationships, her own vision of deity.

Lifting sleepy veils, she provokes, challenges and motivates, pointing out barricades of pride and apathy. She is a teacher of the Craft, a guide and an advisor; in wider society, she is a diplomat and politician, an objector and an advocate. Her skills are many and individual, yet in all she does her magic is in the currents of energy. She wakes others to the power of the web of connection.

Where threads are being ignored, she draws attention to the connections, reminding us how all of nature is linked and related, and how each action affects the whole, the ripples of energy flowing out across the web. Further, where there is no inspiration felt upon those threads, where there is conflict or numb lethargy, she directs the focus to the essence, allowing us again to be touched by the vibrancy of life. Across the divide between ignorance and acceptance, she creates pathways of interest and insight. Where there is confrontation, she crafts a bridge of empathy, showing us the beauty and pain that lie at the heart of each moment. Feeling the energy of every situation, she draws into focus the tangible stuff of creativity and mortality. Teaching us of the power of presence, she recalls to our perception all that inspires us naturally, magically, to hold respect for life.

Earth, air and fire have been touched upon in these pages so far, and here we look to the final element that draws the balance into stability. Although it is to some extent both artificial and simplistic to correlate bardism with air and ovatic craft with fire (most studies in the tradition beginning with the study of earth and presence), nonetheless using this pattern we can see how the Druid works with water.

For where the ovatic fire brings courage, allowing us to express a greater depth of truth, the Druid uses the wisdom of water to manage the force of the emotion. Water teaches us about motion, flow and direction; not containing like earth, or formless like air, water holds yet is flexible, gives freedom yet supports. It can devour, yet, unlike fire, most often transforms gently and with exquisite patience. It cannot easily be pushed or drained. It enables us to learn more about our emotional self, that deep limbic well of human energy so often misused and misunderstood, its resource dismissed as irrational, dangerous and devoid of value.

Questing inspiration, the Druid finds it in the flows of energy, in its rivers, springs and tides, in its crashing waves and trickling brooks. Perceiving the soul's purpose, its drive and direction, finding the beliefs that underlie the emotion, he steps into the flow. Primarily his study turns his focus inwards. As he learns more about himself, he is no longer afraid to feel the deepest emotions that pour through him, and within the security of both his nemeton and the confidence of his intention, he releases sufficient neocortical control to slide fully into the currents. There he rafts the white water, finding critical skills: perhaps most powerfully, he learns the ability to stay fully engaged within his emotional being while not being overwhelmed. He is not taming this force of human nature, suppressing it with great dams, creating toxic reservoirs. Alive with respect for these divine powers within, he becomes a master of this Craft, honing his emotional intelligence.

With each ride, his understanding develops, yet simultaneously he is clearing backlogs of unexpressed feelings. Without the past looming over him, he learns how to use the power of this energy responsibly. Even the wildest currents are not spitting, foaming liabilities, useful only for destruction; nor does the Craft teach him to avoid situations that are provocative and emotive. Instead, the Druid finds inspiration in these currents, learning ways in which he can direct the energy into the poignance of his chosen creativity. Losing the fear of his own deep emotion, of his wild human nature, he achieves a reality that is rich with calm.

The Druid's quest allows her to perceive these flows not only within but all around her – in other human beings, in the flight of a bird, the curiosity of a cat, the hunger of a mouse, the sun-craving of a blossom, the sap's flow within a tree, the dance of the wind, the curl of a wave, the driving of rain, the stillness of a pebble. It is not only what we'd call emotion. What she feels is the momentum of the soul, the flow of energy upon some inherent current of purpose.

It is a quest that leads her to reach for empathy. How does it feel to be a raindrop, shattering on silk-wet rock? How does it feel to be the oak, as the shuddering scream of a chainsaw eats through another branch, or the heifer, in the stench and noise of production-line slaughter or the little girl looking up at the stranger with the chocolate?

Emphatically, once again, this is not to romanticize through anthropomorphization. Projecting our own adult human consciousness, with all its own fears and cravings, on to the ishness of another is, in fact, completely counter to what the Druid is doing. Through the common strands of mammalian evolution, through what we share in terms of ecology and climate, we may think we recognize the behaviour of another creature and label it fear, pain or love. Our preconceptions are notorious; many of them are socially 'normal', built into what is accepted, believed as fact, such as the 'love' of a hungry domestic cat. Where there is less or no recognition, society allows us to treat the creature without a glimmer of respect; the hook is torn from the live fish's mouth, the spider is crushed underfoot, the rat bludgeoned, the forest felled. Reaching beyond the preconceptions, the Druid's skill is in releasing her own consciousness in order to experience and so to understand what is entirely another's flow of energy, another's soul intention and consciousness.

The degree to which she does this depends upon both her level of skill and what is required for a situation. Leaving her human body behind, if consent is given, she may move her consciousness into another's creativity or physicality, taking a ride with a seagull, a fox, a wave or a cloud. Alternatively (this takes more skill), she may use the resource of her own deep memories and of relationships she has forged, and slide into another consciousness while still in her human body, shapeshifting into another form: she becomes wolf or blackbird or gust of wind.

She may be deluded. How can we ever be sure that what we are doing is genuinely, for those moments, taking another's path? We can't. Yet whether or not her own physical form changes is irrelevant (some people believe this cannot happen, while others swear they have seen or experienced such things themselves); the reason she does it is not the hubris of trickery and show. What actually matters is in her mind. It is a part of her quest for inspiration, and in the tradition her success is measured purely by the effectiveness of her resulting work. In finding comprehension of another's soul purpose, she is hoping to spin or awake awareness to threads of connection, and so to inspire the necessary interaction for change. If there is awen in the result, wherever it is she has been, her journey was well done.

In many ways, the practice of Druidry is all about this process of questing inspiration and channelling it through the soul into perfect creativity. A religion based wholly upon nature, the tradition claims no divinely established point to life, no supreme reason for our term on Earth, fraught as it is with crises and pain. Instead of having some worthy purpose given to us by God, it is up to each individual to construct their own. The natural spirituality of Druidry, with its focus on inspiration and creativity, offers us a way of addressing that singularly human demand for a purpose.

I have explored in these pages the deep connection that brings inspiration; creativity is as complex. What we make need not be lasting, or even tangible or comprehensible, but a tremendous amount of our human satisfaction is based on the effectiveness of our ability to create *something*. The closer it comes to an expression of our innermost soul, and the closer it is a reflection of what we sense to be our naked truth, the more satisfying are both the process and the result. More importantly, however, it is the natural pride and positivity cultivated by our creative achievements that nourishes our self-esteem. As our life comes to its close, it is not the heap of things we have created but the inner confidence their creation brings that enables us to die willingly, knowing that we can stand beside our ancestors with dignity. It's for this reason that our creativity has been and still is so central to the Druid tradition.

So much clutters the landscape of our creative expression. Self-negating beliefs lie like the debris of war, and not least are the razor-wire fears of failure and rejection. The more honest our self-expression, the more painfully any criticism is taken, and the worse are the hazards of subsequent self-defences. Yet true creativity cannot be explored without clearing the ground of such barricades.

Some mess is inevitable, the refuse of thought processes discarded along the way, and junk can be inspiring, with broken remnants of forgotten ideas re-emerging as new resources. However, there are times appropriate to pick through rubbish and times to clear the land. Through the cycle of the seasons consciously trodden, the festivals holding us in tune with the natural tide of regeneration, all that is released at the closing of the year is laid down as humus to enrich the soil through its decay. Indeed, the fertility of the soul can well be measured by how fully we have let go of possession of the past and attachment to the future.

New creativity, like new growth, needs a clear landscape. What seeds we have kept to scatter will be as vibrant and productive as the land allows, yet poignantly will be limited also by their own relevance. In other words, the seeds that grow will be those that are nourished by their natural connectedness within the web of that moment in time and place; if their growth is not fed by the threads of the *here and now*, they will fail, however much energy or artificial fertilizer we pour into their care. Forced fertility is not what the Druid seeks, within either himself or anything around him. He does not strive through fear of barrenness.

*Fertility* is a powerful word: the ethereal quality that is needed for our inspiration to germinate, flowing into creativity. In the fields of the Druid's vision, fertility is a most sacred concept. Like a river, with hard work it can be directed, a little, but it can never be pushed. It can be managed, with respect and cooperation, or it can be misused and abused. Where it is forced, the energy is sharp and the land tires quickly.

The sweetest fertility, the most tender source, is always to be found in the wildest places, in the wilderness of our own vision. Here we find an inner landscape untouched and untamed, still devoid of the clutter of past construction and habituated associations. Alive with the rich scents of raw instinct, the unburdened flights of innocence, the spontaneity of hope unchecked, the soul's wild fertility is precious. How we access this catalyst of our creativity without destroying it in the process is a potent skill. Entirely natural fertility can be an elusive force, and one that can prove harder to reach as the years pass, with experience filling gaps of understanding and expectation. The Druid's skill is to rediscover the pathways of the child to this wonderland, in the same way that some manage with old age and as death creeps close.

Yet what is this magical tincture?

Often when we speak of fertility we are looking at a very Christian and childish model: the male and female come together in order to conceive a divine child. The fertility is assumed, a sure gift of God, owing to the purity of an act that he has sanctioned as acceptable: sex for reproduction. Indeed, the aspect of Paganism that is defined as a fertility religion is often profoundly limited by this insistence on male/female union. In the Great Rite of twentieth-century Wicca, the high priestess and her high priest usually invoke into each other specific or gender-focused deities (i.e., '*the* goddess'), and share penetrative sex as a way of enacting this union that is understood to initiate all life. In the last score years, this rite has increasingly been performed symbolically, with the Wiccan community demanding a higher level of socially acceptable behaviour – a consecrated dagger lowered into a chalice of red wine – but still the vision is that of male entering female.

Some areas of modern Druidry have distinguished themselves from Wicca by affirming that the Druidic focus is not on the divine parents, but on the child, the *mabon*: the creation. In my own Pagan Druidry, this still feels too limited. Just as it has been said that technology is manacled by its obsession with the wheel, I feel that magical creativity continues to be limited by this underlying concern with heterosexuality and the bearing of children. Secular society is moving beyond that; Pagan Druidry should be leading the way, for its focus is on neither the creator nor its creation, but on the power of the web's perpetual creativity, the dynamic of every moment's *creating*.

Looking beyond the duality of gender, we dismiss, too, the dogma of cause and effect. Instead, we walk out into the open country of *experience*, and here we find what is the most important word in my understanding of magic: pleasure.

Locked in the knot of mother/father/child, the mysteries of

fertility are not addressed. Just as the core of Druidry cannot accept inspiration to be a force that is entirely erratic, a gift of the gods descending with luck out of the blue, so we can't accept that our experience of fertility comes in the same way. Through the craft of sacred relationship, we can drink the exquisite draft of awen that is our inspiration. Yet it is when spirit touches spirit, and our whole body and soul are awake, that the experience fills us with the deep ecstasy of pleasure, and it is this exquisite pleasure that is fertility. For in our trembling wakefulness to the very essence of life, every cell is open to new potential. Where that is sufficiently infused with honesty, trust and the soul nakedness of perfect intimacy, there is no limit to what can be created.

Whether or not this connection is between a man and a woman is utterly irrelevant. Pleasure comes with deep connection in whatever way we are able to open our soul to the experience. It could be two men that find that peak of divine exchange, or two men and a woman together sharing the ecstasy of complete connection. It could be one woman and the spirit of her dead grandmother. We could find that moment with a soul that is not human, one with an entirely different sense of gender, purpose and consciousness.

It is not necessary for a stick to enter a hole. Magic doesn't come with the poke, but with the ecstasy that is the merging in perfect trust of two souls, the deep pleasure of opening to give and receive. With every shudder of the soul's delight, the surrounding web of connection responds, energy moving in ripples of vibration. The magic of change is a natural result of the experience itself. What we feel is our own creativity wholly interwoven with the creativity of every other soul that is connected into that moment in time and place, every soul involved and witness to the power of its pleasure.

Without the need for the accumulation of perpetual growth, without the claim of personal possession or immortality, the Druid's magic lies beyond the mindset of scarcity. Embedded in nature's tides of life and death, it emerges and recedes. A momentary expression of soul creativity, it is born of the intensely sacred pleasure of spiritual interaction.

Lifting the chalice, I watch the softening sunlight break over the bronze of its curve. For a moment, I feel myself present only to enable this interplay of sun and cup, to witness the opulent sharing of light. Feeling its weight, I lower it and watch, too, as rays play on the liquid, sparkling, glinting, slipping right through, and I'm aware of my own being opening, the cup's warmth in my hands, the dance of each spirit.

'My lord, power of light, for this passing day I give you thanks,' I bow, closing my eyes to the sun, gently letting the day's events play again through my mind. When I open them, the golden ball is sinking behind the treetops on the horizon of the ridge. I raise the chalice to pour a libation onto the dry mud and late summer grass, with thanks, then bring it to my lips. The metal is cool underneath to the inner heat of the whisky, which washes over my tongue with a tingling, seeking burn. I let it linger in my mouth, finding each rich depth of taste, the fumes of its aroma rising from the cup and filling my senses, as I call to the spirits of that sacred place. In my memory, breaking through cloud, the setting sun glances off the water of the loch, a thousand colours of iridescence shimmering off the darkness of its surface, as peat oils swirl and cling in shifting circles around grasses at its edge. I reach down to the black water, and with a fingertip touch the liquid mirror, softer than silk around my skin yet icy cool, feeling the slow, dark ripples of its silent response.

I swallow, my soul wide open, filled with the scents of the island wind upon the loch, and the warmth of that liquid seeps through my entire body, a sacred fire that touches every part of me. And the pleasure lingers with that warmth, holding my soul in an embrace of trust, so that when I open my eyes a shimmering awen washes over me, languidly, and a smile almost breaks into a laugh. I'm left in the silence of a timeless moment of bliss.

*When I stand to close my rite, the usual shriek of nerves is silent, too, softened still by the stillness of the loch at dusk.*

The magic of Druidry is not complicated. Like any miracle, it can happen without us understanding how, and we can spend a lifetime exploring its quirks and logic in order to be able to manifest it for ourselves: we learn how to make powerfully sacred relationships, rich with deep-soul pleasure, within which we can find our truth and express our soul's intention.

In a world taut with human dishonour, Druidic magic is about making a difference. Yet simply by diving into its precepts, breaking through fear, doubt and apathy, finding our own truth, with confidence and curiosity, and so walking the paths in deepening connection, magic inevitably flows. The impossible happens. Thus we live the tradition. Without it, Druidry is no more than a handful of theories to turn over and ponder.

# Chapter Nine

# Freedom: Nature's ecstasy

So often secular culture looks over at me and shrugs, baffled as to why anyone would feel the need to get involved in a religious tradition. When I explain that Druidry is not based on the usual catalogue of pedantic canons and implausible beliefs, outlining the foundation of deep reverence for nature, the gaze becomes a gawp: *so if your perspective is rational, scientific and environmental, why add the religious stuff?*

The answer is that we aren't simply looking for understanding. In our search for clarity about the profound questions of life, knowledge isn't sufficient. To some, knowledge will never adequately explain questions such as why we are here. Nor will science ever satisfactorily express the wonder or respect we feel for the infinitely complex patterns of nature that make up the universe.

A language is needed simply to be able to explore the mysteries of existence, and that language is our spirituality. It needs no ludicrous notions of the supernatural, just words with which we can share the adventure of wakeful living; and sharing is the point, for it addresses that inherently human need for community, the tribal acceptance that affirms we are not rejected and alone. Whether we share our vision with just one other soul or with tens of millions around the world, religious language allows us to converse, bonding through both affirmation and discovery. In Druidry, that dialogue is about exploring with others our ideas and our experience, the essential quest for ecstasy, the problem of action and ethics, and the craving for inner peace.

The focus of Druid spirituality is concerned with our being alive, fully alive and human. It is not about living the 'middle way', a life walked carefully along a line of balance, tucked in, nice and tidy. With emphasis and with certainty, it teaches us how to stand in that place of perfect power and serenity at the very centre of our being, in the middle of our nemeton, within the shimmering invulnerability and immortal energy of spirit. Yet this teaching is critical only in order that we might ever have the *option* to be in that stillness. As important as the serenity is our human madness; knowing how to find that calm centre allows us the freedom to go crazy, heading out to explore the edges of our curious and hungry soul, the depths of our emotions, the exuberance of free expression. For it is only at those extremes that we learn about life, growing from each and every experience, finding the inspiration that enriches and drives our soul creativity.

Druidry is not a spirituality that solely guides us to the light of knowledge and healing. In the tradition, individuality, freedom and choice are far more important than some artificially constructed and entirely elusive concept of the perfect body and soul. Creativity is acknowledged whether born of passion, love, anger or pain, and its muses are honoured. As a part of our journey of discovery, investigating the whole of life, the craft of ritual, casting the circle of our nemeton and using our magical shed all allow us a safe environment where we can delve into the darkest corners of our minds. We can tip out the contents of the oldest battered boxes, those locked and hidden beneath a blanket of moth-eaten wool and dusty cobwebs, without causing unnecessary disruption, hurt or chaos. We can confront the demons in our soul, scream the energy of transformation, dance with the dead and disappear into parallel worlds that make no sense in this one. We can find the child within us, the wizened mage, the clown, the freak; we can be ourselves, tender, beautiful and free.

Some people declare that it's not possible to live in that state of ecstasy all the time, so deeply connected, soul against soul: passion burns out, or burns us out. Certainly, this Craft is not about learning how to run without end. Once again, it's about choice. Knowing we need never be alone within the web of spirit, we can choose to spend time in stillness, integrating, finding congruence in the quiet of our own growth and realization, or we can reach into a new possibility, breathing the darkness of new potential, finding trust that allows us to open the doors of our intimate sanctuary and experience more than we have ever felt before. The wild soul is not insane in terms of being beyond his own control; he is free, and he is free to choose.

That doesn't mean that, selfishly, he can do anything he wants. The way in which we are connected into the web means that the basis for our decisions is completely integrated. Furthermore, the deeper we journey into the living tradition of Druidry, the more conscious we are of that connection, and the harder it is to act without full responsibility for the part we play.

During a radio debate I was recently involved in, a rather sour Christian journalist, who was unable or unwilling to listen sufficiently to comprehend the Pagan view that I was presenting, declared that my spiritual tradition was devoid of reason and, further, that Paganism clearly failed to value that human faculty. His misjudgement was total. In Druidry, without belief in some supreme authority (with a capital *g*) who lays down rules of universal morality, every thought, action and interaction must be wholly considered. With no one preaching what to do, each individual holds responsibility for his own life and creativity, making his choices through an awareness of the web of spirit, with awareness of the emotional tides that are the divine forces of human nature within him, and also conscious of his own free will, held within the power of his human neocortical reason, reminding him that every action or inaction he makes is his own choice.

A profoundly ethical spirituality based on individual choice may not be easy for the monotheist to grasp. Yet this is living Druidry: the quest for that ecstatic pleasure which is at the heart of nature's fertile creativity.

Power games are so integral a part of human society that it can be hard to imagine life without them. It is interesting to consider how much would change were we able to untangle the fear of scarcity and rejection, untying the knots of competition. With no mother/giver/lover to fight, no perpetual rival/threat to vanquish, or a father/judge to submit to, the way in which we relate would be radically different. Simply by discarding that ubiquitous defensive-aggressive attitude, a world built on cooperation would be naturally created. It's a simplistic and utopian idea that can be thrown into theories of international politics and global society, but because Druidry looks to the individual and the individual's relationships, the potential and efficacy of the concept remains entirely the responsibility of the individual. How much does each one of us relate through competition and needless fear, losing opportunities for cooperative creativity? How often do we make interactions that inspire? With awareness, we can each begin to change our own world.

Inspiration comes through sacred connection. When we are able to be open in trust and allow that soul-to-soul touch, our true intention can slide into mellifluous harmony with another's truth, pieces of the puzzle sweetly fitting into place around us. Spirit dances with spirit. Like a wildcat upon a warm rock, merging in trust, interweaving all that we are, there is no angst of competition, just the energy of essence sparkling against essence, shining with awen.

Even when another is no stronger than we are, if their insecurity or lack of respect provokes them to play power games, there will never be enough trust for us to open without risk of harm. Yet, without such caustic play, the poignance of being soul naked with a spirit that is significantly more powerful can be intense, our senses heightened by the limits of our trust being provoked. It may be a deity such as the wind or sea, or it may be a lover who (we feel) has more inherent power, physically or emotionally. The Craft would not encourage us to *submit* to either – god or lover – but there are other ways of deepening our connection further.

Sacrifice is an important concept in many religious traditions, and it has its place within Druidic practice, yet to understand it fully we begin with the practice of honourable offerings. Emphasizing the value of making offerings of thanks, the tradition encourages us to give of our creativity in such a way that we become the muse for others' inspirational flow. We may make our offerings to something that has inspired us, offer it to another person or more widely to the world, but the cycle continues, the Celtic knotwork of interaction, soul creativity inspiring soul creativity. The value to ourselves is simply in the expression, that value measured by the extent to which we are finding our own truth; external to us, the value is in our contribution to the well of inspiration.

Our offerings need, then, to be of our own making, expressing the depth and honour of the relationships involved; I have seen Pagans thoughtlessly picking wild flowers in order to leave them at an ancient shrine, yet without clear connection and consent, these flowers are stolen creativity and not theirs to offer anybody. It is only the expression of our own soul that we share with honour.

There are times when offerings are given not in thanks but before an event: some people may consider these to be deals made in exchange for a god's favour, or even gifts made in order to capture a god's attention. However, the time and energy we dedicate both to making and presenting these offerings is simply a way of focusing our minds into the song of the deity we are honouring. Whether in thanks or in anticipation, we are just affirming the connection.

Making a sacrificial gift is one step further. What defines it as a sacrifice is the fact that it hurts. Our rational mind has made a decision that, emotionally or physically, the rest of our psyche will find hard to carry out. What we are giving is, in part, the pain of overcoming our fear. We are determining to live more fully, at least for a moment, within the flow of that natural power.

The art of surrender, however, is one step further still. When we surrender to a power of nature, the exquisite draft of awen is even richer, for we have sacrificed our control. The spirit to whom we surrender is free to take exactly what it wants of us.

<hr/>

*She'd sat before me with wide eyes, brimming with tears of undiluted commitment. 'I know it's the right thing to do but I don't know how to do it,' her voice shaking with all the surging waves of her emotion. And as I looked into her face, another face emerged, so soft, broken with passivity, a previous lifetime of her soul perhaps, an alternative to her* here *and* now, *the same soul but floating down such a different current. I watched and saw it recede as she stopped waiting for my words, filling the moment with more of her own. 'I know you understand. I've heard you talk about surrendering to Cerridwen.'*

*Here I interrupted. 'No, not to Cerridwen.' The assumption again that, as a Druid priest working with a dark goddess, my principal goddess has got to be Cerridwen. 'And don't confuse dedication and surrender. You spoke of dedicating your life to Bridget, but how much are you willing to give?'*

*As I look at her now, I remember a priest whom I worked with, and the very moment many years ago when, in ritual, he offered his life to Odin. Perhaps if his life had not been torn to shreds since that day, with every kind of brutal loss and painful disappointment, the memory would have faded. I hold the grief of the moment when finally I realized that nothing I could do would help him clamber down from the World Tree upon which he hung. Odin's claim was complete.*

*I remember crying out to the goddess who screamed through*

me when my body was swollen and seething in labour, feeling the force of her power like a dam breaking within me, the tremendous weight of nine months cracking the walls of my body and mind. I'd called to her through the storm of unbearable pain as I slid into the peaceful release of losing consciousness, soundless in my broken body. 'Take what you want of me, but let my son live.' Almost three years later, sitting on the tump of an ancient hill fort, I'd called to her again and, slowly, through the chaos, gathered up my world from where she had scattered it.

When life seems so worthless that we don't believe it can get worse, craving a way to feel more deeply, to experience more fully, it can seem a good idea to give it all to some other force. And when the power moving through us is so strong that it feels easier to give in to it than fight, quite often we do, letting go of our autonomy with sighs of tired relief. With submission, we are freed of responsibility for the steps that we take. I look into this young woman's face and see again the tender emptiness of that other face within her, a face of submission. I'd asked her, 'Do you want to learn how to swim, feeling the power of your own body in tune with the currents of the river, or do you want to learn how to drown, experiencing the exquisite sensation of slow release?'

Love is such a power. It's nature is so extreme that when it touches our soul, inviting us to fall, our choices seem either to cling to where we are, refusing to let it in, or to tumble in, submerging, giving up control, letting it break us. Anger is another such power.

She'd tried to answer immediately, claiming strength and clarity, but her words had become entangled, and in her hesitation she'd realized that she wasn't quite sure. Honesty had washed through her, and her tears had fallen. Through her sobs, after some time, she'd whispered, 'Is it wrong to love so deeply?' Wrong? I had no judgement as to which she might choose. Did my old friend regret making the rite to Odin that had destroyed his life, scraping his soul to its bloody raw and honest core? At times.

I'd explained to her how my goddess of darkness had chosen me, coursing through my soul from the beginning of my life,

*slowly taking more, gifting me with pain and visions. In my late*
*teens I had accepted her, welcoming her, knowing that I could not*
*ignore her, feeling that understanding was my only option. In*
*ritual, in questing, and in those moments of my life when her*
*hands are around my neck, I have learned the art of surrendering*
*into the wild, cold undercurrents of her black water but, as much*
*as I am able to hold it, my life is my own.*

*And she stands here now before the fire, the light playing*
*across her face as if in its flames Bridget were waiting, wondering*
*what she might do.* Come dance with me, *she seems to say,*
*crackling as she devours the wood, laughing inside with her vast*
*hunger, her sharp passion, her boundless fervour. It's beautiful.*
*Even though my whole being ever reaches for darkness, this fire*
*goddess touches me and I find a smile broad across my soul. But*
*how I am touched is nothing compared with the woman beside*
*me. For the first time, both the rite and her learning heightening*
*the level of her perception, the light that plays across her face is a*
*perfect outer reflection of the power that dances within her.*

*Her words are spoken with trembling determination, 'I will*
*dance with you, my lady, for you are the power of my inspiration,*
*the light that guides my way and strengthens my soul. I will*
*honour all that you are, your destructive energy and all that*
*emerges through your fire, of hearth, cauldron and sun, through*
*illumination and transformation.' Placing the bundle into the*
*flames, she adds, 'Accept this sacrifice. Honour all that I am.' And*
*as she says these last words, her body straightens, taller, stronger.*
*The fear dissolves and she closes her eyes, opening to feel that*
*moment of harmony that is acceptance.*

---

The old name for the fourth season of the temperate year was
neither autumn nor fall, but *harvest*, and this is still heard within the
Druid community. The season begins at Gwyl Awst, or Lammas,
around the beginning of August, when the first of the summer
grain is gathered in. Around my home valley, it is wheat that, by the

last week of July, trembles drying golden in the sunshine. Scattered amidst the gold, the scarlet of poppies is a sharp reminder of the brutality about to come, the violent snarl of the combine harvesters that leave desolation behind them. As soon as we are able after the first harvest, we make ritual in the fields, giving offerings of thanks – water, herbs and bread – to the harshly shorn land, hurling our empathy in blood (usually menstrual blood) where the poppies had before swayed in the breeze, and most importantly we make our sacrifice, a gift given in exchange for the sacrifice the earth has made for us. Spending hours in the golden corn, then meditating in the spikes of stubble, I surrender into the land. As I seek inspiration for my path through the months of harvest, the cravings of the land itself fill my soul.

It has become a tradition each Lammas in my Grove for us to slay John Barleycorn, Dry Corn Jack. Made of grain sheaves laid out upon the ground, dressed and honoured with laughter, wonder and warmth, when the time comes the figure is torn apart by the scythe. Into the chaos fall members of the Grove, keening, howling, fraught with cathartic tears, for the loss must be honoured; it is an apocalyptic change acutely felt within the web of spirit. Out of the mess of straw and rags is then lifted up Jack's heart of grain, and slowly the cycle is acknowledged, the alchemy of transforming dry grain into warm bread. It is the only time in the cycle of the year when such an act is performed.

I recall my son's first conscious sight of a crucifix, Jesus nailed and bleeding, ten feet tall; without the numbness of familiarity, it provoked nightmares and confusion. The focus on such a tortuous death was deeply disturbing. I thought about Easter, placed as it is at the time of the local barley harvest, but my son was insistent: 'John Barleycorn doesn't bleed over your altar all year long.'

It's true. At the height of the harvest season, around the autumn equinox, we give thanks for what we are now able to store, the abundance of our land, finding poignant awareness, too, of personal harvest, acknowledging what the past nine months of our own growth has produced. There is no death at this rite. It is a time when we sacrifice our Western complacency, and give energy, effort, money and time, re-establishing a focused connection with the world beyond our pleasure-rich and fertile shores. Giving thanks for what we have, we share it out.

Death emerges again as the harvest tide ends with the Samhain festival, or Calan Gaeaf. Closing the year, we honour the path that travels from there into winter's darkness and death. This is not about sacrifice, though; for at this time of year death comes naturally and it is this natural flow that we honour, seeking to find a way within ourselves that moves in harmony with the environment around us, releasing the dross of the growing cycle now ended.

Just as the focus on light is kept in balance with the dark, so is there no cult around the sacrificial death, perhaps because regeneration is constantly and reverentially acknowledged in the flow of nature.

Content to feel nature's powers within us as we honour them around us, Samhain provides an opportunity for reflection upon our own death. It's a good juncture each year to ensure that our lives are in order, our wills are up to date and legal, and our burial or cremation requests are easy for others to find and understand. Far from being morbid, the tradition guides us to be familiar with the practicalities of death, so avoiding unnecessary confusion when its demands arrive on our doorstep. After all, a person may take years to die, allowing others to adjust and matters to be arrange, but equally someone can be gone in a second.

It is hard to speak about the process of what actually happens at death without using either the poetic language of a spiritual tradition or the limited concepts of proven science. In Druidry, with the acceptance of individual experience and no blind belief required, ideas can vary. My own vision is painted from my years of interaction with the dead, from my work with others as they've moved on from life, from the times when I have stumbled close myself and now, as my physical strength wanes, from the learning that comes as it creeps closer. In many ways, my perception brings science and religion together again: dying is about what happens to the mass of tiny particles that make up our soul consciousness when our physical body gives out.

Retaining its cohesion, that mass detaches from the body. If all is well, it takes (what to the living is) around three days for us to ponder upon what has happened, consider the life that we've lived, make our goodbyes and move on. In trauma this can be done much faster, or indeed it can take centuries and longer, particularly where the soul cannot emotionally let go of an event, place or person. Those who can't detach are sometimes perceived as 'ghosts': souls often calmly existing between life and death, these can also be individuals who are deeply wounded or emotionally disturbed.

Sometimes it is a terror of death that stops a person releasing sufficiently to make the journey, or the chemical imbalance of drugs (opiates in particular) or shock that confuse the mind, but ordinarily these wear off over the course of days or weeks. It is usual for the physical then emotional pain of dying to dissolve completely as soon as we accept the path ahead, and the relief of that encourages us to take the steps needed. Many people see this first stretch of the path as a passage through a dark tunnel, at the end of which is a clear white light; it's an image that relates to the moment when at last we fully allow ourselves to disconnect from the body, our consciousness finally and completely unhooking from the physical form.

The journey on from there is wrapped in the images of what we are expecting, for it is the release of these beliefs that paves the way. We may head towards the setting sun, over sparkling deep waters, or rise up through clear skies, perhaps blending into the patterns and memories of the stars. We may find ourselves in the feasting halls of the gods, in meadows of tranquillity, our soul song no longer cloaked by the weight of physical creativity. We may remain there for some time, finding a new wealth of truth and purity of self-expression. Slowly, naturally, however, we release the last of that lifetime, all imagery fading as we find the emptiness and freedom that lie beyond.

Moving beyond the limitations of time and space is not a linear road, though, taking us off and out to some distant location. It may be an all-encompassing shift in the way that we perceive and interact, but we remain here, there, anywhere, everywhere. The energy of the dead, the soul consciousness of our ancestors, is around us, within us, as much as it is far away. We are still connected.

Present and still in a cohesive conscious state, albeit less defined and contained than when holding a physical existence, at any time an ancestral soul may touch the cells that ignite the moment of conception. Created by the spark of spirit, the awen of such deep contact, the soul establishes its link to the zygote, guiding its development from there. Thus our ancestors become our descendants, and death and regeneration are utterly intertwined.

It can, however, happen at death that our soul consciousness loses its coherence. This is something that happens relatively infrequently, and it seems to occur for a couple of reasons. If a person commits suicide or dies in total despair, the power of the transition and the craving for annihilation can very occasionally be powerful enough to shatter the mind. Destroying its own song, the soul rains each note back into the cauldron of potential. Then again, this dissipation of consciousness can also occur when a soul who has lived many lives with wakeful awareness has no desire to continue its existence as a separate being. Far from involving despair, this process is about total release. Feeling it has reached the end of the long road, in the process of dying the soul unglues its mind, dissolving the cohesion, breaking it up into its subatomic particles, to drift in the wind, in the songs of the trees, in the scent of blossom.

It is impossible to find the soul of one who has shattered in pain, for they exist now only in our memories, but the soul that purposefully releases itself from form is easier to sense, for they appear to be always with us. Without form or linear thought, intention or location, we hear them in the song of all nature, their wisdom richer, clearer and sweeter than ever we heard before.

It is for this reason that the ancestors are such an important part of our spiritual tradition. When we call to our ancestors in ritual and prayers, we may be asking for specific guidance from those who are conscious of our existence and coherent in their form, but perhaps more poignantly we are waking our own perception to their unceasing presence. We speak of their stories humming in our blood and bones, and this is true in terms of our genetic inheritance, yet felt too in the sense of their presence being *everywhere*. We speak of the breath we breathe having been breathed by our ancestors, and in this too we accept the practical logic of our globe's one body of air, yet also in the poetry and omnipresence of their consciousness.

———◆———

*It's a dark turquoise blue, 'the colour of the sea off Iona,' she'd explained, where he had sat for so many long and languid days watching the birds and the waves and his life all softly settling. A round box, she'd tied around it a scarlet ribbon. It holds half his body, burned grey and ground to dust. And I hold it in cold hands, whispering the prayers that flow through me, my mind moving upon that path of deep golden sunlight, over the waters to the west, upon wide and silent wings. There isn't much more to say; like wearing a robe, my words are a formality that is quietly guiding us both into the right frame of mind.*

*At the memorial rite in the forest, she had invited half a dozen close friends. They'd all been to the crematorium a month before, sitting there in the crowd of his own family, distant relations, business associates, vague friends, unfamiliar faces. In the thick of the old forest amidst the dance of falling leaves, in muddy shoes, they had smiled and sniffed, in gloved hands and quietness. And with kohl-smudged tears and tender support, she'd scattered his ashes over the leaf mould, half laughing at herself, self-conscious that he was watching, yet feeling silly with doubt because then again maybe he wasn't. And when I'd raised the chalice of whisky to drink in his honour, I'd seen him clearly walk from the edge of the clearing, smiling with warmth, gently accepting. He'd glowed with love and appreciation, and as I made prayers he'd walked over to her, putting his arm around her. And feeling something around her change, she'd snuggled deeper into her coat, and sighed, closing her eyes into the moment.*

In the last of the twilight, the standing stones loom over us with a gravity of millennia. How many have come to this ancient circle before, this wind-scoured, derelict, lonely place, to mourn their dead? I feel so many around us. I hold my focus on her as she gazes at the ground, just her and myself in the growing dark. I can't see or feel him at all but as a knot of grief within her soul. She is aware that the purpose here is to ease her own need and let him go, and as I hand her the box she grits her teeth in determination.

'Don't try,' I whisper, 'just let it be.'

She nods.

And into the stillness she starts, murmuring his name, over and over, stopping to find breath, reaching for words, until the first flurries of grief's rage are spluttering through her, and suddenly into the night she screams, 'NO!' And sinking to her knees her words lurch over tears, 'Why, baby, why did you go? How could you fucking go? Why?!'

I sit down on the cold, muddy grass, whispering soundless affirmations, holding this sanctuary of her grief, as she sobs, this woman I barely know, and I wonder at the life I lead, the path of a priest, waiting in this moment for her to find a way through. When she does, her words are so tender with love that my own heart opens, a tear rolling down my cheek. 'It's time now . . .' she pauses to breathe through her own tears, '. . . I know that it's time for you to find a new horizon. I always said the most important thing was that you were free, happy and free, with me or without me. Be happy, my love. We will meet again.'

With hands clumsy and cold, she pours the ash from the box over one of the fallen stones. There is no wind and it falls into a little heap of pale grey. She stares at it, then turns to me, 'I'm just going to . . .'

'Sure,' I whisper. 'Take your time. We can close when you're ready.' And I bow in respect, pulling myself to my feet, walking a little way back to give her space undisturbed by my presence. When she feels she's done enough, I'll close the ritual, opening the barrier that I've cast around us, allowing a clear transition *between these moments and life beyond. Until then, affirming the edge of the circle, my job is to wait.*

    *In the darkness, sitting with my back to a stone, I breathe the chilly scent of the coming winter and watch as the dead move amongst the stones. Some are no more than flickerings of faint lights, others have outlines and a few even have faces. Like a hand on my cheek, someone brushes past in the breeze. My bobcat lies beside me, stretched out on the ground, and as I look up to see the soul that passed, she looks up too. I lift a hand and run it through the soft fur of her back; she arches a little, stretching into the pressure, and I'm touched by a deep sense of being in the right place at the right time. It feels utterly natural to be here tonight.*

---

When our Druidic journeys of experience and understanding allow us sufficient learning to glide over the fear of death, when our vision has changed those deep animal drives like our instinct to survive, what is left is not a sense of personal power. The critical shift takes place in our attitude as to who or what is in control.

There is no supreme hero, no divine autocrat in the Christian style, nor a feminist All-Mother loving goddess to take his place. Not even nature is in control, for nature itself has no coherent purpose: it is a web of numerous souls each upon its own journey, connecting, affecting, adjusting as they go, the glorious chaos of numerous patterns in collision and harmony. That is nature's way. It always has been.

As we grow up, waking, learning, our understanding of that changes. We slide from beneath the apparent wrath and hypocrisies of an older generation we feel don't comprehend, gradually instead finding our autonomy, accepting responsibility, fine-tuning our intentions. We find ourselves: an integral part of the web of life.

That change in understanding is reflected, too, in the evolution of humanity. In primitive religious practice, concepts of deity clearly reflected what was deep-seated human fear of the forces of nature.

Subjugated by its storms, floods, freezes and quakes, by hunger, disease, rage and pain, people naturally and submissively revered those powers that lay beyond their ability to understand. The gods were a cruel authority, judgemental and tempestuous, at times merciful then merciless, their divine reasoning as utterly mysterious as the miracle of conception. This is old Paganism, no longer apposite to what the tradition has evolved into. Yet it holds a basic vision of 'god' that persists to this day in many monotheisms.

As humanity developed, accessing neocortical reason, exploring itself and its place in the world, old fears were swept away. Seeking the rational counterpart to the *soul*, ideas about the *mind* emerged. As humanity's sense of its own power grew, the concept of deity adjusted, mysteries crumpling first into theories then into demonstrable science. Forces of nature became resources, objects to conquer. Even the omnipotent capital *g* God was dragged closer to understanding. The ego took centre stage, the same Neolithic human need now looking down the barrel of a gun.

Yet over the past century this too has been changing. Science has brought general human vision down to the cellular level. It is no longer necessary to acknowledge any kind of authority governing from above. The mysteries of existence are still with us, yet the world is not controlled by them. The patterns and structures that are the temples of nature can now be seen scientifically both micro- and macrocosmically, in terms of subatomic and galactic forces. Creation, through the ceaseless creativity of every flow of energy, begins at the level of the tiniest particle, increasingly seen and understood as intention and even consciousness.

To explore spirituality on the microscopic level may sound bizarre. We are looking at the divine neither as a force of nature that can be seen, heard or felt, nor as a sentience that is supernatural. Yet reaching into molecular or atomic level, we can find intention in the same way that we do in a storm or stellar system. This is nature as divine, but it is deeper than the sanctity of life, deeper than animism. For atoms or particles may come together in the formation of life, but are not life in themselves.

Within my own theology and Druid practice, hydrogen for me

is deity, a deity that I melt into, listening, learning, exploring with every new reach of the relationship I forge, within the nature of life and existence without life. The goddess I so deeply honour is in the poetry of all darkness, in the eternal black of the universe that stretches between stars and galaxies, between subatomic particles, between moments and ideas of the mind, but her soul's truth is also expressed in physical creativity as hydrogen. Breathless existence, death, darkness and the exquisite potential of all life lie in her soul.

Oxygen to me is a wild young god, a molecular power of life, vibrant with song and the lust for connection. His dance is euphoric, boyish, laughing, yet his love for hydrogen is utterly devotional, unlike carbon, a dark god, whose relationship with hydrogen is wrought with purpose. A power with exceptional focus, carbon's intent is perfect clarity, measuring and experimenting: he is a powerful force of creativity, whether constructing or destructing. Nitrogen is lush and easily overwhelming, helium a goddess of dreams, both beautiful and harrowing, silicon a god of war, and so the list goes on. But all these are poetic images, and in part playfully presented here in the hope that my words might inspire others to take the vision of their spirituality into new layers of nature.

To trance on this level, exploring molecular consciousness, is worthy of many long years of dedication. Though now the lessons integrate naturally, when I began this path of Druidic study, my vision was altered profoundly.

———◆———

*It isn't that she says* No *to me. She doesn't exist in a specific location, either in time or in space. It is instead a complete wash of negation that saturates the entirety of my vision, including my past and my path ahead, a wave crashing through me that blockades my thoughts completely.*

*OK, I whisper. So show me . . .*

*Already drenched in her energy from the ritual dance, every cell* of my body is heavy with her emptiness, alive with her darkness, billions upon billions of universes soundlessly humming within me, each one reflecting the infinite reach of the universe that is around me, swirling yet seeming not to be moving. Perfect stillness and exquisite motion: I can feel it, I can sense it. The sensation feels like poetry. My brain just can't grasp it. What am I missing?

... Show me.

And as I close my eyes I find myself falling backwards, downwards, into her endless darkness. I feel an awareness that I could stop, at any moment lifting a finger, stretching out a hand, finding the edge and holding on. Or could I? I don't want to try. This isn't like the wild, swirling, gliding, dark descent into the cauldron of death and potential, into the womb of creation. I am not gliding; I am falling. As I release, accepting her guidance, affirming trust, I find that actually I'm plummeting, and any sense of being able to stop is suddenly dashed away. Yet there is no gravity: I'm not dropping but tearing in whichever direction I put my mind to. I try it, skidding sideways, even up, accelerating faster than the speed of light, for I'm conscious of passing other bodies of energy, yet I'm moving too fast to see them. It is exhausting, I'm reeling, dizzy, yet I know, too, that is only because somehow I'm holding on, and again I do what I can to let go, let go ...

The darkness intensifies as I feel her closer, breathing me in, and I wonder at her in-breath, for it must extend for billions of years. I feel sure that I am out in the midst of deep space and, as I wonder where I am, immediately I stop moving. It is bizarre to be still. At first all I see is darkness, then a shimmering of light like an extraordinary electrical storm. My sight clears and I start to perceive pressure. All around me are black bubbles, each one at least five times the size I feel myself to be, some vast, arching over, disappearing beyond my vision. The surface of each is only visible when light shimmers across it, surfaces moving against each other, responding, somehow connecting, sharing energy.

So did I ...? My question is too stupid to be formed, but she hears my intent and in the split second of thinking it, I am once

*again moving, tearing silently through space. I have a sense that
everything else is moving, too, moving around me, with me,
through me, across me. Is this exhausting because I am holding
myself in my own bubble, I wonder, and as I plummet through
space I open my nemeton. I'm not sure what happens first:
incredible pain explodes through my head and she spits me out.*

*A part of me is sitting on the cushions by my altar, acutely
aware of looking out through the shining film of my organic eyes.
But I am also in the cushion, I am in the wood of the altar, I am
looking down on myself from the dark air above. Shattered. It
takes a moment to work out what to do, finding my physical
lungs, breathing, for each part of me feels it is in control. From
somewhere I formulate the intention to come together, then piece
by piece I relax into presence, letting it happen.*

*Bewildered, exhilarated, I stagger to my feet, but they seem to
be sinking into the ground. I watch carefully as I place a foot
down onto the carpet, seeing that it stops, supports, surface against
surface. The same happens with a hand, sinking into the wood of
my altar. Edges are blurred. I fall onto my bed and let my body
sink into the rugs.*

My lady . . . *I murmur.*

Be careful, *I feel her say.*

*Closing my eyes, a taste of a memory returns to my
consciousness. Just before I was thrown from the journey,
everything made sense. Everything. Not intellectually. Not pieces
of an idea neatly falling into place. Nor was it that in that
moment I understood or saw anything. I felt complete connection.
For a split second, I was the web.*

*Lying in the dark of my room, I smile. In the arrogance of my
human soul, I thought I'd felt that before. At the time, I'd been
exhilarated, feeling myself shift down onto a deep level of
understanding. Once again . . . once again, I realize I knew
nothing. I know nothing. And as I breathe deeply and sigh, I
commit to exploring this new vision, aware that one day I shall
feel it to be equally naive. That's hard to imagine now.*

*All I want is to feel it again, to dissolve my self into the*

*tiniest particles of life, to be a billion dark bubbles, to be one, held
in the exquisite anticipation of her in-breath, dancing in the very
soul of nature, shimmering with the song.*

It will come, *she says.*

*I wonder how long I have to wait.*

⟫•◆•⟪

There's something about Druidry that fills me with wonder. In all
that I do, through my teaching, in talks, lectures and presentations,
when some journalist hurls questions, in the rituals that I perform
for myself and for others, in wild celebrations and when the air is
tight with grief and trauma, I do my utmost to infuse my words
and actions with that wonder. At times I feel that I succeed, and at
times, when my journey is heavy around me, I know that it shows
only as a deep glow underneath. Without it, I would have no
motivation to share.

Yet, what you have read here is my perception. The philosophy
and theology of Druidry and the experience of its Craft may be
utterly different for you. Even if you have found moments of
glorious empathy within these pages, your path will still be
different from my own. It is my sincere hope that this flurry of
words scattered in dry ink across these pages has at least been
thought provoking, even if their usefulness only emerges as a way
of clarifying your own vision. In truth, if I were to write these
pages next year, if I had written them before, they would be filled
with different images, for ideas develop and change, as indeed this
ancient tradition must ever continue to evolve. Each one of us is
an exquisitely significant part of that process of change.

What is important is not what I have said, but what you feel
yourself. What is crucial is not what you feel, but what you do,
what we each do. Wild and free, true to your own soul, connected
to the web of all nature, I urge you to live life fully, every moment,
here and now ...

# Index